Evacuation:
A Family Guide for the 21st Century

2013 Edition

Look for our companion book:

Surviving Disaster Without leaving Home

Available through Amazon.com, book stores and on our web sites

WORLD DISASTER REPORT

www.wdrep.com

and

THE DISASTER GROUP, INC.

www.tdgroups.com

Tornadoes across the Southeast, April 2011
A Survivor's Story

"I confess, I've been reluctant to write this. There are some events in life that are felt deeply. To write about them almost feels as though you're trivializing the experience, as though posting on a blog could do any kind of justice to the event you've witnessed. But I write for our family that spent time on their knees, the friends that continued to try calling despite the fact that they weren't getting through, and most of all I write for my children. No one expects a natural disaster like this. You don't know how bad it is until it actually hits. You'll spend the days afterward wondering and wondering some more.

Last Wednesday our area (and our state) was hit by a series of tornadoes, the largest and deadliest outbreak in decades. Our immediate area was hit by 13 tornadoes, some even earning the EF5 rating. .

And now, I write.

"I'd like the refugee special" I told the man at the sandwich counter. He laughed with me as we both looked around the truck stop. People from all around the region were flocking to the first town to rediscover electricity after days of darkness. The gas lines (one containing our minivan) were lined up down the street. The man next to me was mindlessly stroking his week old beard and talking with a friend.

"Did you hear about ____ road? The police have it blocked off until the bodies can be removed." he said.

"Did you hear about the 17 month old?" His friend replied.

I quietly ordered our food, the first "good" meal we'd seen in days. Another man next to me stood up as his number was called for a hot shower. All around me people were swapping stories, who were missing, whose house was gone, and when did anyone think power would be restored to the region. It was comforting in a way to hear news and share information. The last few days had felt like a vacuum- energy and information sucked out of life and leaving a small amount of chaos in its path. I reflected again how strange it was that when you're in the middle of a disaster the rest of the world knows what's going on around you but you are left in the dark – literally and figuratively. I thought about my journal entries of the last few days.

April 28, 2011

Dear Journal,

I suppose I must take a moment to write. There are more preparations to make but I'm so tired all I really want to do is sleep. They're calling this one of the worst natural disasters in the history of the area. At least I think they are, the rest of the nation seems to know what's going on here, it's the people that live here that don't. I find that sadly amusing.

Yesterday we were hit by a series of storms, violent intense storms one after the other. There has been a lot of damage, a number of deaths, and now the entire north half of the state is without electricity or phones. Cell phones aren't working. Nothing like being without electricity to discover how much you rely on it. Nothing like being completely cut off from communication with the outside world to discover how much you depend on it.

Do you know how quiet it is?

Do you know how dark it can get at night?

Do you know you may actually be without power for the next 5 days? Well, there goes all the food in my freezer.

I have so little information. When I woke up this morning and discovered I still had a working radio, how eerie it was to hear

6

there were no grocery stores open, no gas, no drug stores, nothing. What you've got in your house is all you have so learn to make do.

I wish I had rotated the food in my 72 hour kits (portable containers) weeks ago when I had intended to.

I wish I had a car charger for my dead cell phone (not that I could get a call out anyway).

I wish I had a generator to run my freezer (or a small frig).

I wish we had propane for the grill (because of course, we're out).

I wish I knew where the camp stove was and how to work it.

I wish I had more food to prepare that didn't require cooking.

I wish I had more batteries and more flashlights.

I wish I had more paper products (as I now have no dishwasher).

I wish most of all that my husband was here.

He's on a business trip. How I wished he were here as I watched the most threatening sky I've ever seen roll over my house. I wished he were here as I huddled in the bathroom with my children and listened to the storm pound around us. I wished he were here as I was going to sleep in the blackest black I've ever seen. I miss him.

We've had lots of friends stop by to check on us this morning. Never have I felt so blessed to be living so close to friends.

There have been many who've suffered much in the last day. I feel blessed that the Lord has watched over my family. Hopefully we'll get power back soon."

Jessica

To our families
and to all those who may fall
in harm's way

Acknowledgements: We would like to acknowledge the following friends for their contribution to the content of this book Chris, Diane and Ben Goga, for input, Rick Mayson and Keith Doughtery for technical input, to Rick Hodges for some internal images and to the "Editor in Chief": Karen Jones.

Breezy Point, N.Y., Nov. 12, 2012 -- Aerial view of Hurricane Sandy damage to homes in Breezy Point, New York. Following the hurricane, a nor'easter struck the area causing more power outages and additional flooding. Andrea Booher/FEMA

CONTENTS

When the time has come to act, the time for preparation is over!

This book will help you prepare for an evacuation. By following this outline you can assess your risks, plan what to take, how to pack/prepare, how to execute a safe and effective evacuation and if you cannot return home, how to restart your life in another location. This book also addresses the option of not evacuating and how to make sheltering-in-place more livable.

If you are ever faced with the need to evacuate, you will be far better prepared after implementing these concepts. By its very nature and by definition, in most cases, evacuation must be done in haste. In some cases only moments lie between recognition of the need and the time to carry it out. If you use this system of analysis and planning, you will have a great advantage. Great comfort can be felt every day by knowing you have done all you need to do and are ready for any eventuality.

The solution to possible evacuation is sound planning and preparation.

What questions will this book help me answer?

You will learn

- **How to begin** your planning process (simple checklist)
- **How to determine** most likely threats (how to make a simple survey of area threats)
- **How to set up** a simple and inexpensive storage system so supplies can be easily stored and if necessary transported on short notice (how to properly store supplies inexpensively, how to pack containers, how to load your vehicle)
- **How to determine** where to go if you must leave home (how to select a destination, how to make prior arrangements with friends or family)
- **How to plan** if you suddenly become a refugee. What to do when you arrive at your destination (you have escaped the disaster area, but now what?)
- **How to begin a new life** if need be (if your home and job have been destroyed, you will have to start over)
- **How to keep your family focused** and safe during a forced evacuation. Overcoming chaos and avoiding danger is the primary focus of your efforts. Through reasonable planning, and thoughtful preparation, you will more likely be able to move yourself and your loved ones successfully and safely to a destination of your choosing.

Clothes piled in school gymnasium after Hurricane Sandy 2012 – FEMA photo

Examples: **Why plan for evacuation?**

- **October 2012** Hurricane Sandy forms in the Atlantic Ocean, then turns northward to make landfall in New Jersey and New York. Although this storm makes an unusual combination with a cold front, it remains category 1. Storm surge into the bays and estuaries on the northeast coast cause devastating floods, massive power loss, and many deaths. Infrastructure was damaged so badly that utilities were not restored for months in some areas. **Note:** Revised flooding studies had been completed by state and federal agencies two years prior to the event, so no one should have been surprised at the extent of damage due to wind and flood. It appears the Northeast US is still highly vulnerable to such events.

- **August 2012** Hurricane Isaac brushes past New Orleans and everyone breathes a sigh of relief. The news cycle moves on, failing to give significant coverage to 100,000 persons made homeless in lower Mississippi, and whole neighborhoods flooded (4-5 feet of water in homes) on the west side of Lake Ponchartrain. Property damage exceeded 300 million dollars and many of the homes had to be demolished.

- **April 2011**: A mile wide tornado from the deadly April 25 outbreak struck Tuscaloosa and Birmingham, Alabama. So not as widely reported, at least one tornado also struck Huntsville Alabama destroying the electric grid for many miles and damaging the Brown's Ferry Nuclear Power Station. The Nuclear plant was shut down as a precautionary measure. Motor fuel and other supplies were unavailable for fifty or more miles and electric power for most of the city was out for weeks. Hundreds of thousands of households were affected even though they were not hit directly by the storm. The Mayor of Huntsville advised the entire city to evacuate if they were able.

- **March 11, 2011:** an EARTHQUAKE AND TSUNAMI devastated coastal Japan. Deaths number in the tens of thousands, and homeless exceed several hundred thousand. Nuclear reactor safety systems failed in the aftermath of tsunami destruction. Infrastructure was devastated over a wide area making rescue and relief impossible for an extended period.

- **June 25, 2010** GULF OF MEXICO OIL CATASTROPHE (Examiner.com) "As FEMA and other government agencies prepare for what is now being called the worst oil spill disaster in history, plans to evacuate the Tampa Bay area are in place. The plans would be announced in the event of a controlled burn of surface oil in the Gulf of Mexico, or if wind or other conditions are expected to take toxic fumes through Tampa Bay." (this eventuality was never carried out, but was seriously considered)

- **August 28, 2009:** RANCHO PALOS VERDES, Calif.: Residents of 100 homes were ordered to evacuate about four miles from the community of Soledad, in an area of central California north of Los Angeles. The blaze has consumed more than 2,000 acres of steep grasslands, or more than 3 square miles, since it was reported Thursday afternoon. The blaze is zero percent contained. "These fires are still totally out of control," Governor Schwarzenegger told reporters at the firefighters' command post in Lake View Terrace, California. "This is a huge and is a very dangerous fire. The fire is moving very close to homes and to structures... this is why it's evacuation."

- **October 2009:** ATLANTA GEORGIA residents had about thirty minutes to leave before flood waters entered their homes.

- **May 12, 2008: A MASSIVE EARTHQUAKE struck the eastern Sichuan Province of central China near Chengdu, on Monday afternoon (local time). The quake killed thousands, and injured thousands more who were trapped under the rubble of collapsed buildings.**

- **On August 28, 2005, Hurricane Katrina was in the GULF OF MEXICO where it powered up to a Category 5 storm on the Saffir-Simpson hurricane scale packing winds estimated at 175 mph. At 7:10 a.m. EDT on August 29, Hurricane Katrina made landfall in southern Plaquemines Parish Louisiana, just south of Buras, as a Category 3 hurricane. Maximum winds were estimated near 125 mph to the east of the center.**

- **March 28, 1979 -** If the THREE MILE ISLAND plant (or other nuclear plant) today experienced a catastrophic meltdown and containment vessel rupture, people who live within about a 20 mile region of the plant (who are exposed to the radioactive plume) may be subject to the dangers of acute radiation poisoning (with symptoms appearing relatively rapidly) as well as long-term health effects like thyroid cancer. If people are not adequately sheltered or evacuated in a timely fashion from this region and are exposed to high levels of radiation, they could experience severe sickness and possible death within a few days to months. (as subsequently reported by FEMA)

- **August 2005 Although Katrina will be recorded as the most destructive storm (having struck the United States to date) in terms of economic losses, it did not exceed the human losses in storms such as the Galveston Hurricane of 1900, which killed as many as 6,000-12,000 people, and led to almost complete destruction of coastal Galveston.**

- **August 1992 Hurricane Andrew cost approximately $21 billion in insured losses (in today's dollars), whereas estimates from the insurance industry as of late August 2006, have reached approximately $60 billion in insured losses (including flood damage) from Katrina. The storm could cost the Gulf Coast states as much as an estimated $125 billion. (NOAA.gov)**

Remembering history can help keep life in perspective

CHAPTER 1.

PREPARING TO PREPARE

Developing a preparation mindset is the only way to overcome natural human inertia. No one wants to think about leaving home and lifetime possessions behind. If you live in an area of significant risk, preparing before the emergency arises will save your family and prepare you for the transition to your new life. A big storm changes nearly everything.

- Changing how you think takes time, but you must begin somewhere. Begin now. Don't get discouraged, but press on. Develop a new sense of priorities, and put your life in order.

- No plan can fill in all the blanks for you. The template will stimulate your thinking and help you solve YOUR problems.

- Action is the key to success. This book is a practical manual on how to accomplish a very complex life-saving task.

- Family, neighbors, and close friends may be the key to your (and their) survival. Don't wait until an emergency to become acquainted, and maintain close relationships with your family. Don't put off correcting misunderstandings and mending fences. When trouble comes, old grudges and hard feelings hurt everyone.

- Action will stimulate your thinking, and ideas will begin to flow. You will soon cease to fear the prospect of evacuation.

- Action builds strength, and confidence.

- Inaction feeds confusion and despair. There is no need for despair unless you have decided to give up.

- In all probability <u>not every family member will see the need for this preparation</u>, so you have some persuading to do within the walls of your own home. No family can prepare for possible evacuation with one trip to the store and a single dinner table conversation. Even if you have been thinking about this problem, preparations must be made in an orderly manner if they are to have any chance of being effective. Engage all family members in the discussion.

- Think in terms of preparing over a three to six month period. Get a separate calendar and a spiral notebook in which you can write your thoughts, goals, and milestones, and begin today making notes. This can serve as your basic planner.

Organizing and following through on your plan is the key to success.

A few preliminary do's and don'ts:

<u>DO</u>

<u>Do</u> read and re-read this book in the context of your family's situation. The more you ponder the questions, the more ideas and solutions will come to your mind.

<u>Do</u> discuss how it makes sense to be prepared just in case. Not everyone has to have the same vision of the need. If you can persuade each member of the family to do even a little to help think the problem through, you will be successful. Talk to your neighbors, friends, but above all talk with your family.

<u>Do</u> buy a small notebook and begin to make lists of things to do and purchase.

<u>Do</u> become familiar with your geographic area in detail, what routes to avoid in case of gridlock, and consider ALL alternatives. Note transportation routes, lakes, rivers, bridges, and other obstructive features. Knowing these now will prevent confusion later.

<u>DON'T</u>

<u>Don't</u> become discouraged and quit or lose interest. In-depth planning and preparation takes some time.

<u>Don't</u> invent your own wheel. Check local sources for suggestions and available assistance. Cities, counties, church groups, and FEMA have highly informative web sites (we have provided links in the appendix). Many municipalities have employees who would gladly discuss family preparedness with you in person. They know that the citizen is really the one who has the most likelihood of success if properly prepared.

However, they tend to view things from an institutional response viewpoint because that is their job.

Don't think that your preparations mean nothing, or that the task is too large. Start with small tasks and keep working on it.

New Jersey Hospital badly damaged in Hurricane Sandy shows interior walls gutted - 2012 FEMA photo

CHAPTER 2

HOW TO ASSESS YOUR MOST PROBABLE THREATS:

Put first things first and begin to improve your long term situational awareness. Ask yourself: What existing factors might threaten family security?

Our lives are flooded with information, however many people live apparently oblivious to the condition of the world around them. Increase your situational awareness. Regularly sift relevant information sources and keep them in mind. Your preparations for the most likely threats will also serve you well in case something unexpected occurs with little warning.

Suggested Action:

a) Your county is required by federal law to have a Multi-Jurisdictional Hazard Mitigation Plan. DMA 2000 (Public Law 106-390) provides the legal basis for FEMA mitigation planning requirements for State, local governments. Read your county plan to assess your local risks.

FEMA link http://www.fema.gov/plan/mitplanning/guidance.shtm

b) Make it a habit to regularly read and compare **reliable** news sources, and not depend on the daily television news (which often lacks meaningful content and is mostly entertainment) to tell you what is important, and about what you should be concerned. Use your head to determine most likely hazards.

c) After you have identified the likely hazards <u>for your geographic area</u>, stay informed about those risks by frequenting reliable sources (for example: if you live within 250 miles of Yellowstone, you can determine the condition of the volcanic caldera by checking the United States Geologic Service Yellowstone website (http://volcanoes.usgs.gov/yvo/) Your local Emergency Management Agency (county, city or both) will often post information relating to hazards as they develop. *This is where the media gets its raw information before they turn it into uninformative drama.*

Assessing most probable threats in your area

When trouble comes, the problem is where you live. Each situation, each locality presents its own set of unique problems. The local Emergency Management Agency may provide you with a basic list of threats, but they can't list them all. You must do some work.

Do your own investigation but keep it simple

- Research the history of your locality on line.
- What kind of reoccurring problems has your area experienced (tropical storms, earth movement, heat/cold)?
- Do you think your neighborhood would likely be safe, or would it be a powder keg?
- What does your city or county Emergency Management Agency suggest are local threats?
- Now that you have some information, what do YOU think are the most likely threats? Make a short list and discus with your family and neighbors.

Of the major disasters you uncovered, which are most likely to require evacuation? If you don't live in an area where these are likely threats, evacuation may be less likely. The following examples are presented in no particular order, and remember that your area may have threats that are not included in this list, but are just as serious.

Common Sense Danger Zones

- Within 5 miles of a railway line, interstate, or major state highway corridor (transportation accident)
- Within 10 miles of a military base
- Within 10 linear miles of large chemical manufacturing, tank farm, or storage facilities (industrial accident or sabotage)

- Within 50 miles of a nuclear power plant (industrial accident or sabotage)
- Within 75 miles of known active seismic zones, including presently dormant major fault lines (seismic activity)
- Within 75 miles of the coast (hurricane, tsunami)
- Within 250 miles of a semi-active volcano (seismic or volcanic activity)
- Anywhere on a 100 year flood plain
- Within 50 miles of a dangerous urban area (any urban area might become dangerous under adverse circumstances)

Are These Dangers Found In Your Area?

Highway or Other Transportation Corridor (are you within 5 miles of railway line or major highway)

The advent of terrorism and the statistical probability of highway accidents make problems in this area somewhat likely.
- may be no warning at all, and the risk of occurrence is relatively high
- hazardous materials travel over roads frequently (much more than we'd like to believe)
- a highway or railway accident may produce an event of monumental proportions depending on conditions

Military Base: a military base may have very hazardous materials stored, or may be a target for nuclear, chemical, or biological attack.
- may be no warning at all, but location is more secure and the risk of occurrence is relatively low
- an accident in a military munitions or chemical storage area may produce an event of monumental proportions depending on conditions

Active Seismic Zone

You should be very wary if you live in an area of known seismic disturbances. Seismic zones are more predictable than most other hazards. You should consider yourself to be in a seismic zone if you live within 50 miles of a major active fault, near a dormant volcano, or within any of the known danger areas such as the extensive New Madrid Seismic Zone that crosses several states and is the epicenter of the most violent earthquake ever recorded in North America.

- Possibly not much warning (if any) before a major earthquake
- Actual area of maximum danger (damage) is not known before the actual occurrence (past epicenters may have little or no relevance to the next one)
- Being able to evacuate "early" is not probable since everyone gets the evacuation "message" at the same time (i.e. when the event occurs)
- Be able to leave within the hour if you can find a road out of town. Get as far as you can as fast as you can. If you know the epicenter location or axis of damage, head away at right angles. Don't head into/toward the epicenter even if the roads appear to be intact in that direction. Aftershocks may occur, destroying roads that were previously passable.

Large Chemical Manufacturing, Tank Farm, or Storage Facilities (industrial accident or sabotage)

- Industrial accidents are more common than you know.
- Chemical facilities often have warning sirens. Don't ignore those noises.
- Most industrial security is inadequate, making them highly vulnerable to sabotage or outright attack

Nuclear Power Plant (industrial accident or sabotage)

- How would you know if an accident occurred? What warning system is in place to alert citizens in close proximity to the installation? Can you hear or see the warnings if an accident were to occur?
- What are the most reliable media outlets (local radio stations will probably get the word very early in the emergency) in case of accident?
- What direction do the generally prevailing winds blow? Do you live up or downwind from the facility? Do you know how to minimize radioactive contamination, and how to avoid ingesting it and how to clean it off?

Proximity to the Coast (hurricane, tsunami)

- Depending on terrain, a tsunami can reach many miles inland from the coast.
- 100 miles from the coast is still quite close where a hurricane is concerned, but should be out of danger in case of tsunami.
- Being early to evacuate is a matter of your judgment and clear thinking. Everyone gets the evacuation "message" at the same time.
- Does your area have a tsunami warning system? If so, do you know how to recognize an alarm if it is activated? Do you know the main and alternate evacuation routes?
- Do you know where you are heading if you evacuate? Have you made arrangements for temporary shelter with family or friends?

Hurricane/Tsunami Zone

According to USGS, 50% of the US population lives within 50 miles of the coast. A hurricane could strike anywhere from the Gulf Coast to New England. If you live in these areas, you need a thorough understanding of the threat, and good plan. Tsunami risk is higher in many nations bordering the Pacific, and while these events are not frequent, they can be catastrophic in scope and duration.

Japanese earthquake and tsunami damage (US DOD photo)

Volcano (seismic or volcanic activity)

Volcanic activity is fundamentally unpredictable both in duration and intensity. Scientists <u>may</u> be able to predict what type of lava flow is most likely; however there can still be ugly surprises. If you live near an erupting volcano, you need to leave.

- Volcanic eruptions are relatively rare, but often deadly when they occur. Think ahead and follow your instincts. It is much better to leave early and return after a minor eruption subsides than to become part of a modern Pompeii or Herculaneum if the eruption turns out to be "the big one".
- Remember that statistical estimates of times between eruptions represent historical data and are not predictions. When the magma begins to move, history becomes irrelevant.

Flood Plain

Floods are better understood in modern times, but many citizens live in denial of flood danger even though they live in areas that have previously been submerged. If you live in a flood plain, consider moving to higher ground.

- Formally designated flood plains are well known and defined by government and insurance companies, however other areas susceptible to <u>localized flooding</u> and understanding that fact is mostly a matter of common sense.
- Even if you live in a low area (not designated a flood plain) if a hard rain results in your front yard becoming a lake or if the neighborhood topography all slopes toward your front door, It is only a matter of time before enough rain falls to bring about a worst case scenario. Think about your locality and plan for what might happen.
- Consider your situation and don't continue to reside in a hazardous area.
- Heavy rain is not an instantaneous event. If you live in a canyon, valley, or low area keep the weather in mind. Remember that it doesn't have to rain directly on your area in order to flood you out. If it's raining heavily "uphill" from your location, you may get the run off.

If you experience a flood without flood insurance you will lose everything. No government or corporate entity will replace your property.

Common flood scenarios

- In-flux of rain sets up flood conditions (combination of prolonged thunderstorms, slow moving wet weather system, or hurricane dumps excessive amount of water either directly on, or "uphill" from you. (This threat is periodic and if you are vigilant at least you can be forewarned).
- Dams pose particular danger since they may fail for a variety of reasons. Do you live below one?
- If you live in lowlands downstream from a dam, the threat is ever-present (you should consider moving).

Wild Fire Area

- Wild fire depends on sufficient fuel and prolonged dryness.
- Fire conditions are watched closely in fire-prone areas. Your Emergency Management Agency (EMA) will be watching this hazard closely.
- If your EMA posts fire warning alerts, take heed and prepare.
- Even a nearby fire will usually allow some time for an orderly evacuation, but only if you are alert to surrounding conditions.

Dangerous Urban Area

Population density can create highly unpredictable dynamics during times of power loss, societal disorder (political of social upheaval), or disruption of the normal supply chain. When supply lines are interrupted and the populace begins to feel hungry, behavior of the "masses" can become very dangerous.

- Cities can be extremely dangerous during periods of civil disorder. There will never be enough police to control a large armed mob. Leaving for a predetermined safe area is the only option if rioting occurs.
- Riots often "burn themselves out" in a matter of days. If local infrastructure damage is not excessive, you may be able to return within a short period of time.

- Maintaining contact with responsible neighbors will help you maintain situational awareness, provide a possible warning of trouble (don't necessarily wait for civil authorities to declare a problem), and provide mutual assistance as trouble unfolds.

Local officials review flood damage during recovery phase

CHAPTER 3.

WHAT EVACUATION REALLY MEANS

Evacuation from your home is by definition chaotic. Depression, despair, defeat and death stalk the unprepared. The occurrence of a disastrous situation and threat of impending evacuation will quickly disorient even the most emotionally steady and clear thinking individuals. In this setting, logical priorities become distorted, simple factors are badly misunderstood or forgotten, and comprehensive thinking becomes impossible. Evacuation without prior planning is analogous to going into battle without training. Evacuation epitomizes uncertainty and evokes confusion to a depth and magnitude most people have never known. We live in an increasingly uncertain world.

Evacuation options (what are your choices)

1. **If you are unprepared your only option is to just walk out the door:** Just leaving home is not complicated if you leave everything behind as you walk out the door. Simply walking out means that you lose the ability to direct your life.

2. **Wait until someone else (government or someone on TV) tells you it's time to go, tells you where to go, and what you need to get there:** Elected officials and their advisers will probably do what they always do, that is to wait until the last possible moment to make a decision. They have reasons for this behavior. If they order an evacuation and the storm goes elsewhere, they are criticized. If they fail to order evacuation and the storm hits, they will be criticized. There is no way to predict what they will decide, or when they will release that information.

3. **Understand the situation, and be prepared to execute the most reasonable option in a timely manner. You may have a great plan, execute it well, and find out that evacuation was not necessary after all, but your family may be much better safe than sorry. Decide before hand to take responsibility for your decisions. Err on the side of caution and safety for your family.**

Your Evacuation Decision sequence

- When a threat arises, <u>assess the immediate situation</u>. What do YOU think is going on, and just how serious is it? Evaluate it with your family. Don't put your trust in public information statements from civil authorities. In some cases they are not entirely accurate due to changing conditions, lack of information, or political considerations that confuse their response.
- <u>Decide on a timetable</u> with a departure time certain <u>if</u> the threat seems to remain or is increasing. Better to leave days early than wait even one minute too long.
- <u>Assume that nothing you have planned will go just as you have planned</u>. Be prepared to improvise.
- <u>Notify family</u>, assemble everyone who will be in your party at the rally point, and review the plan in detail. Stay together at all costs. Notify your intended host of your intentions as far in advance as possible.
- Load your per-packaged supplies in the vehicle and depart together for your <u>pre-selected destination</u>.

CONSIDER THESE THREE LEVELS OF PREPARATION

This huge LP gas cylinder erupted from being completely buried beneath ground level.   FEMA photo

Short duration (a few hours to ten days) example: a
warehouse fire liberates clouds of potentially toxic (but not persistent) smoke. You have to grab the family, pets, and what you can carry and leave immediately staying away until it is controlled and the smoke clears. Your personal property may be damaged, but no long-term pollution of the earth or water in the affected area occurs. You can go back home, find things pretty much as you left them, clean up, and carry on as before. Infrastructure such as utilities, highways, bridges etc. are not seriously damaged, and continue to operate at a reasonable capacity.

Long duration (ten days to several months) example: a
section of your city riots, burns, and loots, the volcano erupts, the "big" earthquake occurs, the hurricane runs over your location. Personal property is heavily damaged or completely destroyed, the earth and/or water is polluted so as to be hazardous, and if you went back home you

might find it destroyed or so badly damaged that it would be uninhabitable. Utility and transportation infrastructure is heavily damaged or permanently destroyed. Civil disorder may be an issue since municipalities may no longer exist in the affected area. You may have to deal with the National Guard/police if you attempt to reenter the area.

Permanent (you cannot go home again) example: except

perhaps to scavenge the ruins, your home is not habitable, even for temporary improvised shelter. Utility and/or transportation infrastructure is heavily damaged and inoperable, and the area may be under protracted martial law, lawless, or a perimeter under tight police control requiring entry permits. Even if you are a property owner, authorities may not allow you back for any reason. In this case also, whatever other name is used on the nightly news, you are a refugee.

REMEMBER

- **GATHERING THE FAMILY:** this is one of the most difficult things to do well. If the disaster is impending and time is short, every family member must be assembled quickly at home so preparations can be made. **Rally points** are designated so family members know where to go if normal communication is impossible.

REMEMBER

- Communications is the first thing to break down during a disaster. There is no substitute for all family members knowing the plan so they can make an effort to meet even if they are separated and cannot talk to one another.

REMEMBER

- No matter what items you do take, if members of the family have been left behind, your life will be forever changed. Have a plan to collect and account for everyone before you go!

REMEMBER

- You cannot know before the emergency occurs where each family member will be, what transportation options will be available, or whether direct communication will be possible. Cell phones are wonderful devices, but are not operable in a variety of scenarios. You must devise a basic plan to gather the family to a rally point even if a lot of things are going wrong.

REMEMBER

- When the family is gathered, each member must carry out their individual assignments so no one member is forced to make a multitude of decisions (thus becoming a choke point in the work). Parents must cross check each other so important tasks are not omitted due to stress.

Rally points are intended to assemble the family in preparation for the actual evacuation. Movement to a rally point is not the actual evacuation except in the case where the situation is too drastic and no other plan will work (fail safe/last resort). Everyone must know the address (and phone numbers) for the rally locations. The secondary site should if at all possible be at a "friendly" location (a close friend or relative's home where alternative support might be more likely).

Plan to have <u>Three Rally Points</u>

1. **Primary:** <u>Right outside of your home</u> in case of a sudden emergency, such as a fire.

2. **Secondary:** <u>Outside of your neighborhood</u> in case you can't return home or must flee your neighborhood. Your primary destination is your goal, but what if that is not reachable for some reason? Have a secondary destination (in a different direction or area of the country) in case the first becomes impossible to reach for any reason. The ability to shift destinations depends on route planning and having previous arrangements made with potential hosts at those locations.

3. **Fail safe/Last resort:** possibly <u>100 miles or more distant</u>. Use of this scenario presumes that the whole region has been disrupted, communications and transportation are inoperative. Remaining near the home region may be imminently dangerous and the original family evacuation plan is not viable. The last resort scenario is <u>very</u> dangerous for families since it considers the fact that children and adults may be separated from other family members and may have to make their way to this destination through their own ingenuity. Ideally, the fail safe location should be at the home of a very close friend or relative who would be inclined to work from the

other end to help the family reach their location if someone became separated from the main group.

During your planning, visit the first two rally points together as a family and rehearse how things will work until the plan is clear in everyone's mind. Don't just tell family members about the plan; discuss it until they really understand. Ask for and encourage questions. Take extra effort to assure that all family members understand the instructions. Discuss the fail safe scenario as a family so everyone will have the opportunity to sense how serious an evacuation could become.

Volunteers serve meals to victims who lack resources – FEMA photo

Rally points have no value unless family members understand that they may have to make independent decisions to save their own lives. The rally point is intended to accomplish two main objectives; assembling everyone in one place, and gathering all possible pre-positioned supplies for use during the evacuation.

When the family actually begins the evacuation, hang an **ID card around each member's neck or put it in the "go bag"** (or both -see specimen card on page 106). This ID may help reunite family members even if the one who is separated has been injured or cannot communicate with rescuers.

Other Options

Returning Home (or not): once you evacuate and civil or military authorities secure an area, your property rights are abridged. After you leave, you cannot re-enter until you are told it is allowed. **If possible, try to stay at your home**, even if in a tent in the back yard. If the home is too unsafe to live inside, you can still salvage items that may help you as you await the restoration of order. Link up with neighbors you already know and trust.

Living in a Damaged House: Even if your home is heavily damaged (holes in the wall, leaking roof (but not severe structural damage that might result in actual collapse), you should consider staying. If you have prepared by storing tarps or heavy construction plastic, you can often nail or staple barriers that will make at least a few rooms habitable. Staying home means you can look after your property and more fully utilize whatever supplies you may have on hand. Depending on the area, looting may be very likely. Neighbors banding together can often discourage outsiders from committing crimes in your area. Continuing to occupy your neighborhood will often deter criminal encroachment.

Get to know your neighbors before trouble comes. They are probably very good people and will welcome your friendship.

Security Issues: during the unfolding of a large-scale disaster your common sense will be the most effective means to maintain security. Understand that while police and National Guard troops are tasked to maintain the law, their ability to do so depends on the magnitude of the problem, their numbers, and the rules under which they are ordered to operate. Many cities have experienced riots, and in some notable cases (Rodney King trial: riots – 1992 Los Angeles) police retreated because they were not able to stop the disorder, established a security perimeter, and merely attempted to contain the problem within a geographic area. **This approach was of no help at all to persons trapped within the**

danger zone (some of whom elected to remain and defend their property and families). Your planning should include provisions for a hasty departure.

Ash fall from volcanic eruptions threatens all life, machinery, infrastructure, and electronics – USGS photo

PLANNING YOUR DEPARTURE ROUTE

Which Road Should You Take: being creatures of habit, most everyone will attempt to evacuate using the largest highway or interstate, therefore traffic gridlock is inevitable. The whole city/town will be trying to use the same main roads. No amount of police waving traffic on will eliminate gridlock when traffic reaches a certain density. When it comes to directions, GPS is fine if the satellites are functioning properly, **however** include a (paper) road Atlas in your kit so you can determine where the county/secondary roads lead, where they are located and how they connect. In some areas, terrain features will limit your choices (mountain passes, lakes or low areas).

Plan alternate routes to leave your area.

Sometimes it is necessary to head in a less traveled direction in order to get clear of the danger area. Be flexible in your planning. Do not put all your trust in GPS even though they are convenient (and habit forming). In most cases the GPS picture is too limited for you to be creative and consider many alternatives if your original travel plans fail for some reason. You may be forced to take secondary roads in another direction, and then work your way back onto your original course once you clear the worst of the gridlock.

It would also be a good idea to store enough fuel to supply one full tank for your evacuation vehicle. Fuel storage can be tricky as gasoline has a fairly short shelf life. Its life can be extended by the use of fuel stabilizers or the containers can be rotated into regular use to keep it fresh. In some more urban areas there is no place to safely store fuel particularly if you live in an apartment, townhouse or condominium. If you have the opportunity to have more than one vehicle, consider one of them being a fuel storage unit itself. A vehicle that rarely or barely runs can always maintain a full fuel tank. Consider well in advance how to siphon its fuel into empty portable containers and transferred to the primary vehicle in case of emergency. Even a non running vehicle can be used for this purpose so long as the longevity of the fuel life is considered. Of course, if you are lucky enough to have an evacuation vehicle that runs on diesel fuel, it is much easier to store and keep a backup supply. The useful life of diesel can be a year or two, depending on how it is stored.

Mass evacuations create mass congestion and often immobilize interstate highways for tens of miles. In many cases evacuees have run out of gas and/or patience "on the road". Major roads are jammed with everyone going the same direction - OUT OF TOWN! Be prepared for this and develop a predetermined alternate route

It is certain if you wait to leave until the main evacuation has begun, you will become trapped in the mass of procrastinators and lose your options.

HOW FAR MUST YOU TRAVEL TO REACH SAFETY?

It depends on the threat. Hurricanes can reach more than one hundred miles inland even though they are breaking up. Do your homework on possible destinations. <u>Look in every direction from your home and assess the possibilities</u>. One week in an over-priced run down motel will be a lot more livable than one week in a tent or languishing in a public shelter. If you are in a border area, do not cross into a neighboring country without the proper documents or you may be arrested (or worse) by those authorities or possibly be blocked from reentering the country.

- **It makes no sense to flee the coast only to be caught in a low-lying area or flood plain subject to further flooding.**
- **Don't evacuate through or into an area more dangerous that the one you just left.**
- **Think about terrain you will have to traverse, what is uphill from you (water runs to low elevations) and possible escape routes.**
- **Normal escape routes may be blocked. You need alternatives. You <u>must have a hard copy map</u> to review all possibilities (a GPS might not do that for you)**

MARTIAL LAW - CIVIL DISORDER - RIOT

<u>Habeas corpus</u> is a concept of law, in which a person may not be held by the government without a valid reason for being held. A writ of habeas corpus can be issued by a court upon a government agency (such as a police force or the military). Such a writ compels the agency to produce the individual to the court, and to convince the court that the person is being reasonably held. The suspension of habeas corpus allows an agency to hold a person without a charge. Suspension of habeas corpus is often equated with martial law.

Because of this connection of the two concepts, it is often argued that only Congress can declare martial law, because Congress alone is granted the power to suspend the writ. The President, however, is commander-in-chief of the military, and it has been argued that the President can take it upon himself to declare martial law.

Congress may decide not to act, effectively accepting martial law by failing to stop it; Congress may agree to the declaration, putting the official stamp of approval on the declaration; or it can reject the President's imposition of martial law, which could set up a power struggle between the Congress and the Executive that only the Judiciary would be able to resolve.

In the United States, there is precedent for martial law. Several times in the course of our history, martial law of varying degrees has been declared. The most obvious and often-cited example was when President Lincoln declared martial law during the Civil War.

Throughout United States history there are several examples of the imposition of martial law, aside from that during the Civil War.

Hawaii was placed under martial law in 1941, following the Japanese attack on Pearl Harbor. Many of the residents of Hawaii were, and are, of Asian descent, and the loyalty of these people was called into question. **After the war, the federal judge for the islands condemned the conduct of martial law, saying, "Gov. Poindexter declared lawfully martial law but the Army went beyond the governor and set up that which was lawful only in conquered enemy territory namely, military government which is not bound by the Constitution. And they ... threw the Constitution into the discard and set up a military dictatorship."**

On 8/26/2005, in the wake of Hurricane Katrina, New Orleans was placed under martial law after widespread flooding rendered civil authority ineffective. The state of Louisiana does not have an actual legal construct called "martial law," but instead something quite like it: a state of public health emergency. **The state of emergency allowed the governor to suspend laws, order evacuations, and limit the sales of items such as alcohol and firearms. The governor's order limited the state of emergency, to end on 9/25/2005, "unless terminated sooner."**

There have been many instances of the use of the military within the borders of the United States, such as during the Whiskey Rebellion and in the South during the civil rights crises, but these acts are not tantamount to a declaration of martial law. The distinction must be made as clear as that between martial law and military justice:

deployment of troops does not necessarily mean that the civil courts cannot function, and that is one of the keys, as the Supreme Court noted, to martial law."

- Martial law means that local government is no longer functioning due to a disaster, and military support is required to maintain order.
- A formal declaration may not be necessary to invoke martial law, however the appearance of National Guard or US Army troops on the street is a de-facto statement that such a condition exists. Soldiers (National Guard etc.) usually don't want any trouble.
- Remember that the Guard personnel come from among your very neighbors who have donned the uniform of our country and are operating under orders from the Governor of your state or the Federal Government.

Source: U.S. Constitution Online
http://www.usconstitution.net/consttop_mlaw.html#examples

Several New Jersey transit trains heavily damaged and out of service following Hurricane Sandy flooding – FEMA photo

National Guard troops rightly expect that you will obey their <u>lawful</u> orders. These soldiers are fellow citizens, and are usually not inclined to take forceful action unless it appears necessary. Expect them to stand their ground and not to be persuaded by your complaints or arguments. They may be just as nervous and fearful as you.

- They are not likely to be interested in your opinion of their orders. Unless you cause trouble, you will not likely be arrested or forced to leave.
- Martial law means that military personnel are in charge because regular elected government cannot function.
- When normal civil government begins to function once again and order can be kept, martial law should simply cease and be replaced by normal civilian governmental functions.
- Soldiers can and will tell you what to do. They have the authority to act within the limits of their orders. If a very widespread chaotic situation in play, their orders may be open to interpretation and possible error.
- Don't expect all of their directives to necessarily make sense in the context of your wishes/needs.
- They will be following orders issued by state or federal officials who are probably doing the best they can, but have an incomplete knowledge of your local situation. Soldiers are not social workers, and though they are probably good at heart they will not be inclined to debate the logic of their instructions (as is often portrayed on TV).
- The safest approach is to do as you are directed and don't get into confrontations.
- They can arrest and hold you (or worse) if they believe you to be a threat. If they feel threatened by your actions, they may react in a manner that will result in your injury or death.
- Be polite, use your head. They don't want to get rough with you, so don't give them a reason to do so.

CHAPTER 4.

WHAT TO PACK (SHORT TERM, LONG TERM), AND HOW TO PACK IT

- **Go bag (also known as 72 hour kit)**
- **Long Term Evacuation System (LTES)**

Preparing the family for the possible eventuality of evacuation from scratch can become a daunting task. There are several scenarios to consider. We will review the steps one at a time. The **"go bag"** is something that you would have with you in your car **always.** It may have to be carried for a considerable distance. Therefore a small back pack is most suitable. If a situation arises where your automobile becomes unusable (for whatever reason) and you have to get home or to a rally point on foot, it would be there for you. You don't panic because you are prepared. You have a plan in place to carry out whenever is needed. The fact of the matter is that in many cases (if not most) emergencies occur when you do not expect it. That is OK, because that's life; however, it is not OK when it happens and you are not prepared. This is when people make poor decisions out of fear and panic.

Go Bag – a portable container filled with basic items that would sustain the individual for two or three days of foot travel under adverse conditions if necessary. Protection from the elements will save your life. Heat, cold, rain, snow, and combinations thereof are equally dangerous in their own ways. Preparations are mostly common sense.

CONTENTS OF THE GO BAG

As mentioned earlier, you may need to evacuate without first going home. Being prepared with a small supply is better than nothing. If your journey may require foot travel, you must plan accordingly. For most people, the prospect of (for instance) a 100 mile hike (2 hours in a car) is daunting. Think it through, decide what you would have to have, and pack contents accordingly.. Store it in your vehicle and hopefully you won't have to carry it far. However if you MUST walk, make it something you can carry. You might also consider a small collapsible wheeled cart onto which you can attach the pack if you are walking on a road or other firm surface. A radio (see communications Chapter 8) HAM or GMRS, FRS or CB is also very useful.

Suggested packing list for three-day forced march (when you <u>must keep going no matter what</u> until you reach your destination): <u>keep the weight of this pack no more than 10 – 20% of your total body weight. The lighter the better!</u>

<u>Water:</u> pack at least one gallon of water. You will need one gallon each day to avoid debilitating dehydration. One gallon will give you 24 hours to find two more gallons to carry. Modern back packs often have water bladders built in. Carry two collapsible plastic containers that you can fill or several smaller bottles with filters or water purification tablets. Check your local camping or sporting goods stores for those items.

<u>Food:</u> This food is for emergency only. On the march you will need calories to fuel your (soon to be aching) muscles, and keep the items as light as possible without cooking. MREs are a sensible choice. We suggest that you not rely only on jerky since it is lean and often salty. To keep you going you will need fats and carbohydrates. Dried fruit or fruit/grain bars are tasty and nutritious. Chocolate is a good supplement, but a mess in hot weather. Bring enough for six meals.

<u>Prescription drugs:</u> as needed to be physically active for 3 days.

<u>Clothing:</u> change into traveling clothes before beginning evacuation if possible. Wear comfortable shoes (sneakers, hikers). They must have already been broken in! Include two changes of underwear *rip stop* pants, poncho, three changes of socks, two t-shirts, down or poly filled jacket <u>with</u> waterproof breathable shell, floppy hat with brim and (warm) gloves.

Fire starters: Carry all of the following: matches, flint and steel, and butane lighter. Purchase a yellow or orange lighter and secure it with a lanyard to it to keep from losing it. Also carry fire starter paste or a small sealed film can containing cotton balls soaked in petroleum jelly. They will make excellent fire starters.

Flashlight and spare batteries: LEDs store well, are light to carry and have good life if you are careful. Wind-up flashlights are good as well.

First aid kit: Carry only a small basic first aid package. We recommend self-adhesive bandages, 4X4 gauze pads, antibiotic ointment, burn cream, Kling roll bandage, Aspirin, Tylenol, Advil type analgesics, baby powder, *mole skin*, assorted band aids.

Toilet paper: remove the cardboard tube and flatten the roll to save space. Store in a zip lock freezer bag.

Lip balm: You will become dehydrated, and this will help.

Sun screen: SPF 30 must be used to be effective.

Fishing-line and hooks. In case it takes you longer to travel than you have food, the fishing line can also be used to make a snare if necessary.

Parachute cord: at least 50 ft (15 m). It is hard to have too much!

Duct tape: Store in zip lock bag.

Personal items: Soap, toothbrush, toothpaste, and floss. Personal hygiene is essential for survival.

Garbage/Plastic bags 2 (30 gal): Can also be used for a poncho, extra zip lock bags can waterproof anything!

Sleeping bag: or cold weather pants that can be connected to the jacket

Compass and topographical map: of every county you'll traverse on the way to your primary or alternate destination. Learn how to use a compass and *practice the techniques.*

Pepper spray or other defensive items: use your own best judgment, and remain within legal limits.

Pencil and paper: You can leave notes. If necessary, or make them as needed. These would be good to place in a zip lock bag for waterproofing.

Multi-tool and sheath knife: these typically are equipped with a screw driver tip, blade, saw tooth file, can-opener, reamer, and wire cutting/gripping jaws.

MRE (meal ready to eat) at least one so you don't have to cook one meal (six meals would be better).

Emergency whistle for signaling: your voice may give out fast.

Other convenience items: tent (dome type is easy to set up in a small area, and may not require lines and tent pegs) one small aluminum pot with lid, utensils, alcohol stove, GPS, compass and GMRS/FRS (2 meter HAM is best) radio transceiver, 8×10' tarp, compact survival plant reference guide, survival knife, military folding entrenching tool or small shovel.

Cash (Small Bills): It is always a good idea to have some cash stashed away. It may be a good idea to have $1000 cash in a secure location that could be quickly accessed if needed. We suggest $200 in ones, $200 in fives, $200 in tens, $400 in twenties. There may be no credit card machines running when you must purchase necessary supplies in a hurry from someone on the street or other unconventional locations. You need to expect that no one will be giving you change. This is why it is important to have small bills.

Note: See Page 105 for an itemized list.

A tree completely destroys a roof. The home is now uninhabitable.
FEMA photo

LONG TERM EVACUATION SYSTEM (LTES)

The following items are intended to be transported in one vehicle with the family during evacuation. For long term absence think in terms of portable containers, not suitcases or back packs – more volume is necessary to contain supplies sufficient for a long term or permanent evacuation.

LTES = Should fit into a <u>maximum</u> of 5, "PORTABLE CONTAINERS" (3 preferred)

Portable Containers are anything that you can store supplies in. However the criterion is that it should be no bigger than you can pick up by yourself (fully loaded) and preferably water resistant. Many varieties of these can be found in home improvement or large retail stores. The plastic ones with lids work great. Just remember that they may be tossed around a bit and should hold up to the strain.

The ESSENTIALS is a small pack (separate from the go bag) and kept <u>under direct control of an adult</u>. It should include personal identity and other critical papers, emergency cash, basic fire starting items, 1 MRE each person, 1 liter water each person (in case the family has to move fast and must leave the foot lockers behind for some reason).

- **PERSONAL INFORMATION:** convert your information into 3 forms or media if possible, CD or flash drive in common word processing format (MSWord, or Open Office), paper (place copies in 1 gal (doubled) freezer bags to protect from exposure to moisture). Paper is the last resort; don't depend entirely on electronic format. A computer may not be available to read or reproduce your data. Also note that electronic media deteriorates when stored and may not be readable unless you refresh it once per year.

- All of these should be in one place preferably in **one bag, folder, briefcase, or file box** that can be quickly removed and included in the evacuation materials.
- **Make a written list in advance of the precious items that cannot be replaced so you can be sure to pack them.** Not everything you own is "precious". Make this list with wisdom, asking yourself what items would really be missed (or badly needed) in a year or two if you no longer had them.
- Know exactly where these items are and carefully plan how you will quickly gather, efficiently pack, and load them.
- Practice this plan a few times and see how long it takes, if your packaging plan is adequate and how well the predetermined procedure worked. The "precious items" should be packed in 15 minutes. Remember you have other concerns that cannot be ignored or superseded by this component of your planning.
- Write yourself a note and tape it to the top of box number 1 so you will be reminded when you begin actual evacuation

Suggested personal papers:

- Your resume and references (on paper or electronic media) – you may need to get a job before the mass of evacuees the people flood the resettlement area.
- Homeowner, automobile insurance policies.
- Birth certificate, social security card, citizenship papers if you are naturalized. These are critical and should be kept on your person or under your constant direct control at all times.
- Family contact list on paper (names addresses, phone numbers)
- Professional certificates (degrees, licenses, transcripts).
- Back-up copies of your computer hard drive files (time permitting, consider bringing the hard drive with you), laptop.

Portable Container Number 1: shelter (tent) and sleeping bags or blankets, tarp, rope and pegs to set up camp to get out of the weather immediately if necessary. Include 100' of 5/50 (parachute cord) and a package of long bungees with hooks on each end. In some cases it may needed to set up a large fly (using the tarp) and then erect the tent beneath that outer shelter. This approach tends to keep the tent cleaner and other gear less exposed to the weather. Also include hammer and machete for set up and branch trimming.

Portable Container Number 2: food, water, basic clothing, walking shoes, basic medical kit.

FOOD: enough to sustain life for 10 days (three meals and one snack per day). Plan simple meals using nutritional items that require little or no cooking. Keep the meals simple, use as few pans, utensils, and dishes as possible to diminish post-meal clean up. Travel to your destination may not be as swift as you hope.

WATER: due to weight and volume, this is most difficult of all. Pre-pack two gallons per person (bottled water is OK), but in addition carry empty collapsible containers sufficient to fill an additional five gallons per person immediately during travel and to be refilled again once you arrive at your destination. No matter where you go, you will need water. Use your judgment as to how much water you carry. Hot dry weather will dehydrate travelers quickly. Guard against that situation.

Note: Depending on the number of persons and composition of your group, this volume of water may be very difficult to store and transport. One alternative is to obtain a potable water purifier and/or purification tablets to treat questionable water sources you may pass while in transit. Stopping to obtain water could be dangerous depending on the circumstances so consider this alternative carefully. Filters will purify "dirty water" but the consumer must beware that the water is not "chemically contaminated". Filters do not remove all contaminates. These filters can be purchased at sporting goods and camping stores. Even if you have filtering equipment it is be advisable to carry a reasonable supply of water until you reach your destination.

CLOTHING: Evacuation is not vacation, and in some cases exposure to the elements will be a serious factor. Long sleeve non-cotton blend, drip dry shirts can be rolled up above the elbow if the weather is hot, or rolled down to the wrist if wet/cold or to protect from sun or insects.
 Trousers should also be blend, drip dry fabric (beware of cotton because it stays wet, and wicks moisture thus increasing the risk of hypothermia). If you live in a cold climate, consider wool for at least half of your clothing. An extra T-shirt or two can provide convenient and effective layering options to preserve body heat. Don't forget one set of gloves for each member of the group.

Portable Container Number 3: Reserve clothing, job interview clothing, extra soap, toilet paper. **Four days of clothing** allows time to do laundry twice per week, yet not have to carry a large volume of clothing around. Pack this clothing in a vacuum-shrink bag or fold carefully when pack in a plastic trash bag and compress it until as flat as possible.

- Shirts: 3 long sleeve for work or travel.
- Trousers: 3 sturdy weight for outdoors.
- Underclothing (top and bottom): 5 pair.
- Shoes:1 sturdy pair for walking or manual labor,
- Hat: baseball or boonie-type cap for protection from sun, and sock type to conserve body heat if cold
- Socks: 6 sturdy (for walking or warmth), 2 dress
- Mosquito netting in case you have to camp out impromptu

Portable Container Number 4: support supplies (extra large tarp, nylon rope, camping utensils, matches etc).

Portable Container Number 5: whatever else you think you will need to start life over somewhere else (make your own list).

Motor Fuel: If legal and possible maintain basic storage on your home premises of at least 20 gallons (in 5 gal. approved containers) or one full tank of motor fuel, and enough empty fuel containers for one additional tank full. If you have adequate warning and time to fill the auto or truck from the gas station prior to leaving, and you are able to fill the empty fuel containers, you will then have 3 tanks of fuel (one in the vehicle and two in approved containers). Never carry gasoline containers inside a closed automobile. They can be safely carried on a trailer or the bed of a truck in a manner that allows NO FUME BUILD UP. Calculate roughly how far that much fuel would take you if your average speed were 10 mph. Remember that if you wait too late to begin evacuation, your average speed will be more like 2 mph, and you won't get many miles before you need more fuel. You cannot allow your fuel tank to run dry and be stranded in a strange location.

Note: Fuel can be stored in approved containers for varying lengths of time. When treated with fuel stabilizers (available at local stores), gasoline can usually be stored for 6 months and diesel fuel can be stored for a year or longer. Work out a reasonable way to keep extra fuel. It can be stored in approved containers in a well-ventilated area (not your garage), and rotated through normal use in mowers, and your vehicles. You should have enough fuel on hand to get you and your family well out of the danger area. As you travel, re-fill your fuel tank at prudent intervals if gas stations are open. Don't use your own reserve fuel unless/until absolutely necessary.

Note: Some localities may have non-ethanol fuel available. This stores much better than 10% ethanol motor fuel when treated with the same stabilizers.

Consider doing without the air conditioner. Use of AC will decrease your mileage by 2-5 mpg and that could mean the difference between safety and disaster.

It would always be a good idea to rotate the fuel. Over time, gasoline will degrade to the point it is no longer useable. This issue can be averted if you use what you have stored on a regular basis. Use the "first in first out" method and you will always have fresh fuel ready when you need it.

Acquire supplies on a time table.

Make a simple list and buy the items over a specified period of time. Purchase these first, then begin to use your imagination to acquire other items that you feel will be necessary. It's YOUR evacuation, so retain ownership.

Japanese Defense Forces clear tsunami debris. Only heavy equipment can be used to clear such debris. JDF photo

CHAPTER 5.

HOW TO PACK IT

The container size must fit the need and contents must be packed in logical sequence

An important note concerning Go-bags and 72 hour kits

- Your go bag (kept in your automobile) is intended to enable you to reach a more secure pre-planned destination. Seventy-Two (72) hours passes swiftly during an emergency, so remember that these are nothing more than stopgap items in case of real trouble.

- Example of how to pack the go-bag: stays in auto at all times with enough provisions for the passengers to "get home" on foot (or to pre-designated "Rally Point").

- The go-bag should be small, no heaver than 10-20% of total body weight for each person. Shoes and socks suitable for hiking should always be in the car along with emergency clothing appropriate to the general conditions of your environment.

Below: A full pack go-bag. This unit had a waist strap support, and water bladder

Note water drinking tube from bladder carried in pack

JONES

Reflective strips (may be covered if concealment becomes

Full size back pack with waist support strap. There is no need to carry more

Photographs of how to pack portable container (what do you want on top so you can get it as soon as the container is opened?)

- How much do you pack for how many people to evacuate? Plan on specific items for each person. If you are taking a pet, you will need supplies for their maintenance. so they do not become a greater liability.

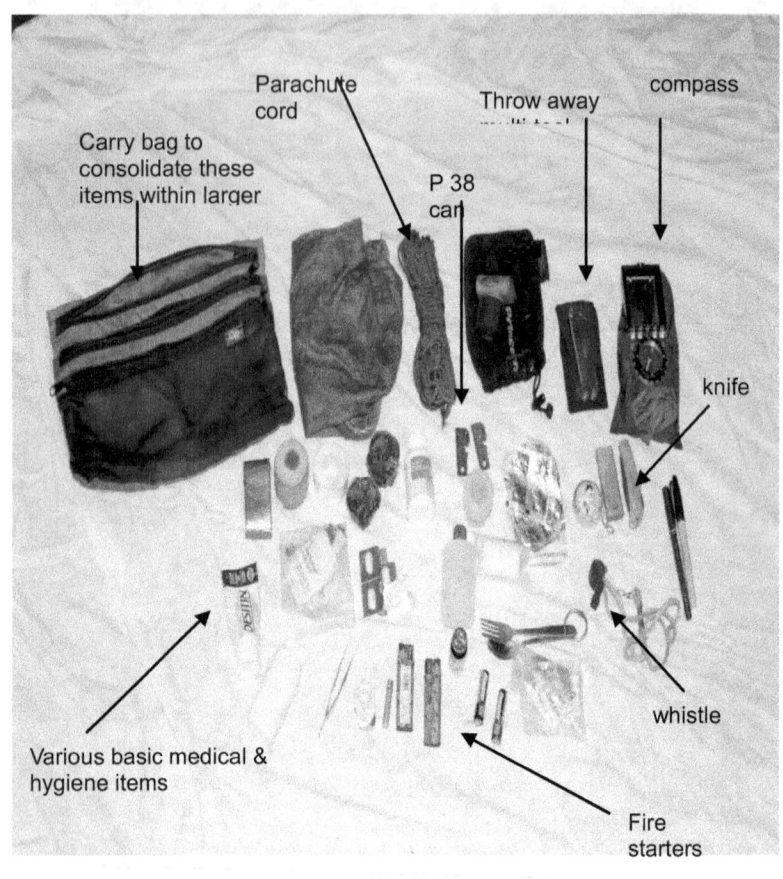

Medical items, throw away poncho, compass/ (what if GPS doesn't work when you need it), batteries, utensils, writing items, insect repellant

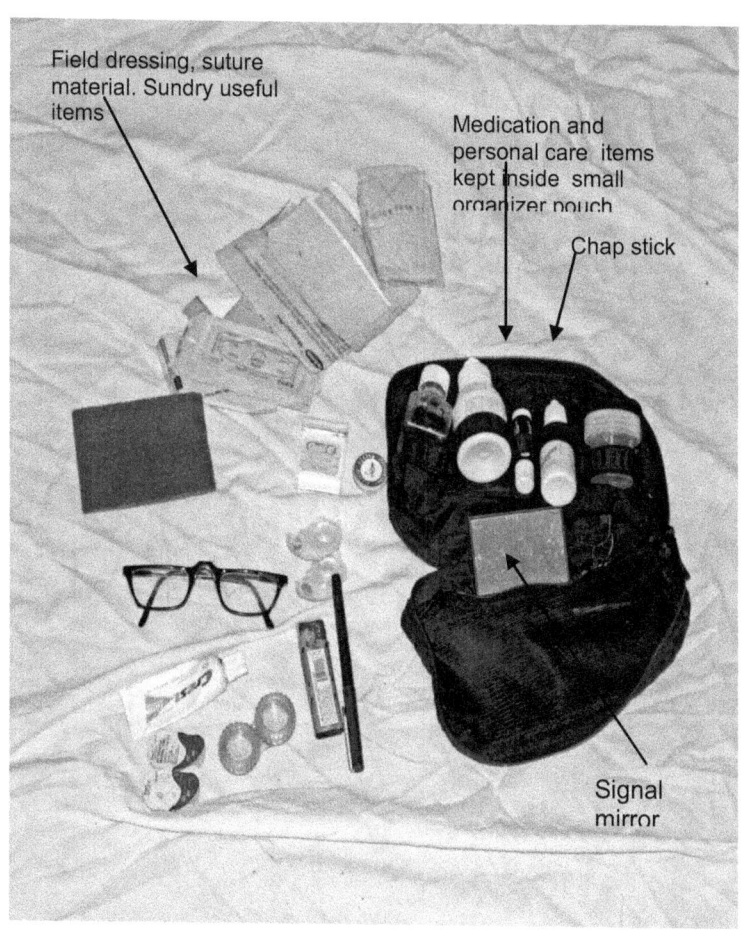

Field dressing, suture material. Sundry useful items

Medication and personal care items kept inside small organizer pouch

Chap stick

Signal mirror

More medication and useful personal care items

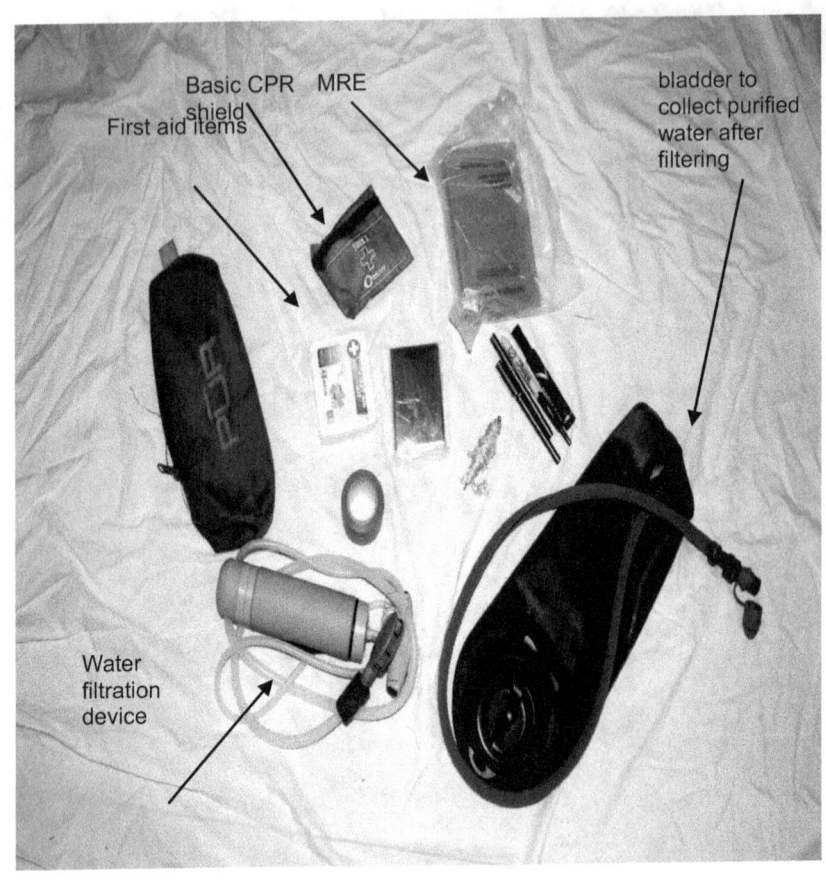

Water purification filter/pump, MRE (at least one meal), container to collect purified water

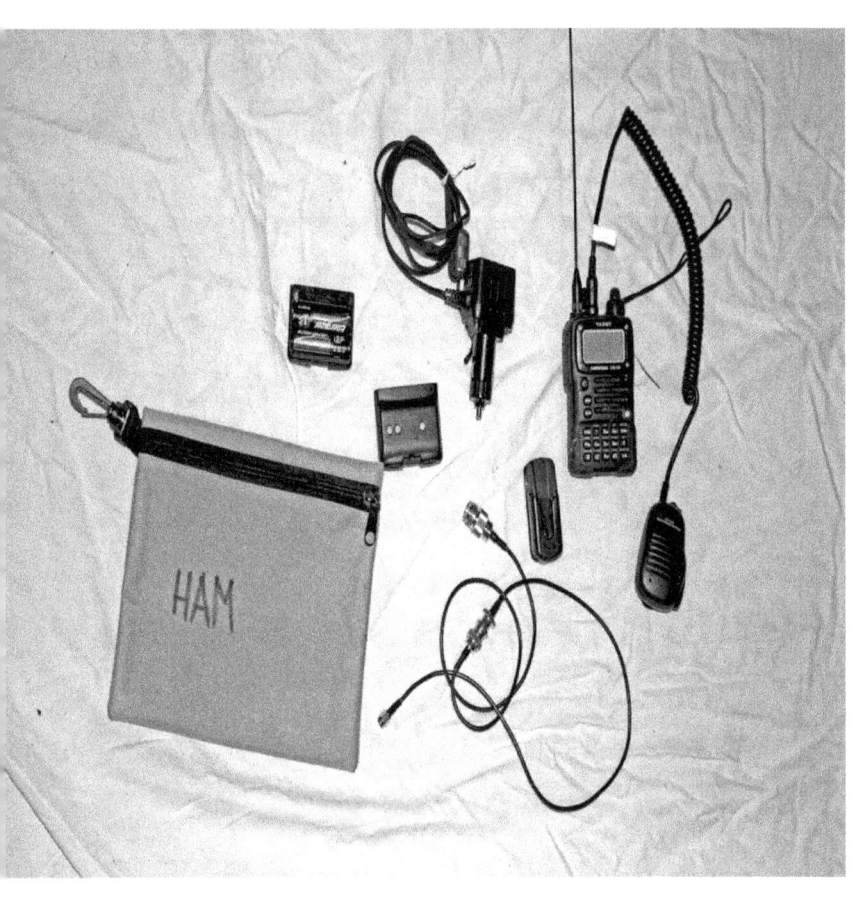

Communication is essential in all emergency situations. Be sure you include this element in your evacuation plan. Give yourself as many options as possible.

Larger plastic portable containers can be purchased from any home improvement store suitable for essential items that can be quickly transferred from a storage place to the vehicle for a quick exit.

Mark the general contents of each box on the outside where it can be easily read. Include an inexpensive light source in each container.

CHAPTER 6.

CHOOSING YOUR ULTIMATE DESTINATION

Evacuate to where?

- During your planning phase, we recommend that you make prior arrangements by checking with the following connections:
- Relatives or very close friends: (don't wait until the emergency to discuss the possibility of coming to live with them)
- Just Friends: (you have to decide how close they really are)
- Acquaintances: some of these may be helpful and compassionate, however don't count on it
- Hotel/Motel: how long can you afford to stay there?
- Camp out in a refugee facility or park: you are at the mercy of government (or lack thereof), and the chaos that often accompanies such gatherings.
- Destination planning must be discussed and agreed upon by ALL parties involved, both evacuees and potential hosts. They should include Primary Destination (D1), Secondary destination (D2), and emergency/fail safe (D3). Remember, these are destinations not rally points. In the case of civil disorder or disease outbreak, safe areas may not be obvious; therefore destination planning must be thorough and flexible.

If you become separated, train your family members to return to the last place they were together and STAY PUT! Someone would return to find them. If that was not possible, they were to STAY PUT anyway until they were found. Most times, trying to find each other at the same time makes the situation worse and increases the distance. Search teams know it is easier to find a stationary object than one that is a moving. In the "worst case scenario" however, continuation to the rally point or predetermined destination independently would be the only other option. This is why it is so critical for EVERYONE to know every aspect of the plan and to be equipped to carry it out independently if necessary. Of course, with children this is another subject all together. Just be careful! Teach these procedures to everyone in the family, especially the kids and rehearse them so they will know what to do if the time comes.

Note: Use the CB or HAM radio to monitor local information. Do not reveal your location unless it is necessary for some critical reason. Listening is much more informative than talking.

Remember that everything you say over the radio can be heard by anyone who has the right equipment and is listening.

Beware of persons attempting to stop you on the highway. Do not speed, because that allows less time for you to make decisions when conditions change or trouble may lie ahead.

What if the worst happens during the journey (death, severe injury, separation from loved ones)?

- **Death:** If the situation demands, you may be forced to leave your loved one's remains and push on to your destination.

- **Severe injury:** your family's movement could be delayed for a very long time in this case. Remember that a complete and satisfactory resolution of the injury or illness might not be possible. It might be necessary for you to get what treatment is available and push on to your destination. Medical help might be more available once you leave the immediate danger zone.

- **Separation:** Don't allow this to happen as it could become your worst nightmare. Keep your group in close visual contact, and remember that normal rules ("don't worry dad, I'm just going around the corner and I'll be right back") do not apply. **Separation could be the catastrophe that destroys the whole family.** Stop right where you are until the separated member is located and recovered.

- **You may need help** finding a lost family member, so start asking for local authorities for help immediately. If no authorities are available you will have to improvise. **Don't get into this situation!**

- **Carry recent hard copy pictures** of the family, and <u>close ups of each member with enough facial detail to allow easy identification.</u>

- **Each family member wears a family communications/ID card** (around neck inside clothing). Print and encase in plastic (even a zip-lock bag provides sufficient protection for a 3X5 card). Thus, even if they are not conscious, they can be identified. It is important to have the important phone numbers written down on this card. Having numbers stored in the cell phone may not do any good if the cell phone is not working.

- **Car breakdown** (keep your automobiles in good running condition, carry extra oil, replacement belt(s), water, duct tape to temporarily repair radiator hose leaks, brake, and power steering fluid). If you break down en route and cannot continue, you are in real trouble. **You don't want to be leaving the family alone with a broken down car while you go for (what you hope will be) help.**

- **Car-jacking, criminal assault,** common sense protection measures (visually check the area before you stop and park your vehicle). Do not park in a manner that requires backing up if you want to leave in a hurry. Most importantly, if something looks out of order at the location you are considering, just keep moving. Be particularly cautions about allowing children or women to move away from the vehicle where they cannot be protected.

  If the primary route is not passable (road washed out, blocked by authorities etc.): you must have a **paper atlas** or map so you can consider alternatives. Remember that GPS is only useful if the satellites are in good order, no other electronic interference is present, and the programming is complete. You should not trust your GPS to properly represent spatial relationships like a map. Have a hard copy map in case the GPS malfunctions. A regional or national road atlas is not expensive and will be valid for years even though minor details may change.

  If you learn that your original destination is no longer going to receive you, divert to somewhere else. This presents a serious problem. That is why you need to <u>carry</u> address and contact information of any possible alternates. Knowing where you are going, how far it is, and who is waiting for you reduces fear considerably.

SECURITY ISSUES: stay out of threatening situations. You cannot "win" a fight while your family is exposed and also being threatened. Escape is almost always a better option than battle when your family is present. Always have an escape plan and a last resort defense plan in case escape is blocked. This "unpleasant" contingency must be discussed with the family so everyone understands the basic plan. Don't count on police to rescue you. They may be occupied with other problems and severely under staffed.

HISTORICAL NOTES ON EVACUATION BY AUTOMOBILE

The Houston Texas example (this report taken from post disaster assessment by the Houston EMA): Common problems during evacuations:

All of the following are observations about the failures of mass evacuations by automobile, based especially on the well-documented evacuation of Houston, which occurred with considerable advance notice of the threat from Hurricane Rita. **It is assumed that future evacuations of major American cities will also be performed primarily by automobile.**

Factor #1: The Bullwhip Effect: The 100-mile traffic jam on the roads extending north from Houston was inevitable, due to the bullwhip effect. As a chain of cars accelerates and decelerates, the longer the chain, the greater the change in velocity at the end of the chain. This is due to the same effect as the cracking of a bullwhip; while the end near the user's wrist may only speed up and slow down a little, the opposite tip is moved through the speed of sound (thus creating the trademark "crack" of the whip).

Future evacuations could resolve this problem through the use of pace cars and rolling roadblocks throughout the evacuation path. These pace cars could help reduce the impact of sudden changes in velocity by building a smoother flow of traffic, rather than allowing the buildup of a conventional urban traffic jam.

Factor #2: The Chute: Very much related to the bullwhip effect is the problem of removing people from the evacuation as it is completed. The 100-mile traffic jam was created as virtually everyone in the evacuation line tried to get from Houston to Dallas. The problem is that this <u>extreme concentration of destination</u> meant that any problems absorbing the extra traffic north of Houston were felt all the way back through the evacuation line...creating repercussions throughout the 100-mile line. On the way to Dallas, traffic evacuating Houston via Interstate 45 passed through Huntsville

Future evacuations need to "overshoot" the target destination. Instead of sending people to Dallas, the evacuation should have sent them beyond Dallas, and then absorb them back into the city. The same principle is in effect at any 5k or 10k road race or cross-country run. Runners don't stop moving once they cross the finish line; they move through the "chute", which is a long lane that absorbs them in an orderly manner well past the actual destination of the finish line. The chute allows large numbers of runners to cross the finish line almost simultaneously without landing on top of one another or backing up just a few meters from the finish line. **What any mass evacuation needs is a "chute" of its own -- a method of absorbing the inbound evacuees at a high rate without congesting the evacuation lanes.**

Factor #3: **Concentration Instead of Diffusion** Northward routes out of Houston: The identified evacuation routes for Houston all points north. While the logical destinations in the event of a hurricane certainly are to the north of the city, that doesn't mean the smart way to get there is by pointing all evacuees in the same direction. This is a lesson that the computer industry knows well; the Internet isn't designed to send all data in the same geographic direction, but instead spreads out the data packets at first, and then lets them re-aggregate once they reach the destination. The same principle is behind Oracle's claim that their grid server "never breaks": Instead of relying on single one-way flow of information, the array of servers adapts to handle computing requirements by distributing the load in many different directions.

<u>Future evacuations need to first disperse all of the people, then let them find their way to the destination.</u> The Houston evacuation routes instead created a massive set of northbound bottlenecks, leaving traffic flowing at ridiculous paces as slow as just one or two miles per hour. Instead, Houstonians should have been scattered in all available directions at first -- northeast, north, northwest, west, and southwest -- then directed northward. Other mass evacuations must do the same whenever possible -- diffusing the people out before their concentration threatens the evacuation itself. **Even an extra hour or two of <u>travel in a direction</u>**

<u>other than north</u> could have moved lots of people out of the city faster.

Factor #4: Dependence on Multi-Lane Roads In response to the Houston evacuation, many people will call for more and wider express highway routes out of the city. Yet Houston is already one of the most highway-heavy cities in the country. An increased dependence on a small number of arterial evacuation routes won't make future evacuations better. Part of the trouble with multi-lane expressways is that they limit the number of available alternatives when something goes wrong. Many of the vehicles leaving Houston ran out of gas, and any vehicle that becomes an obstruction makes for serious trouble on a controlled-access roadway like an Interstate highway.

<u>Future evacuations must use smaller highways and two-lane roads as primary modes of evacuation</u>, just as much as they employ expressways. The worst backup that ever emerges on a two-lane road is caused by a slow-moving vehicle, like a tractor. But on a two-lane highway, a tractor can pull over to the side of the road or onto a secondary road, even if only temporarily, in order to let the other vehicles pass. By comparison, a stranded vehicle on an expressway creates a choke point. A well-organized evacuation must include the use of all roads out of a city, including secondary highways and smaller-capacity roads. A two-lane highway can have its opposing lane temporarily reversed and serve about as much traffic as a conventional two-lane expressway -- but only if the authorities are innovative enough to apply such a practice. An investment in better secondary highways (possibly including timed stoplights or better on-the-scene police guidance) would probably be much more efficient and effective at improving emergency evacuations than simply adding more lanes to existing arterial routes.

Illustration: Using Secondary Highways As Evacuation Routes

Evacuation by freeway alone:
Suppose the city of Des Moines, IA was evacuated, with a destination of Omaha, NE. Interstate 80 is a four-lane expressway linking the two cities. But concentrating the entire evacuation on I-80 would inevitably lead to the kind of congestion (grid lock) experienced in Houston.

Evacuation by multiple highways:
Clearly, the use of alternative routes, including the <u>many two-lane highways running east-west</u> between Des Moines and Omaha significantly increases the potential volume of traffic that could be moved out of the city. If even a few two-lane highways were used, they could rapidly equal the capacity of the Interstate route and temporary lane reversal could increase this capacity even more. This further illustrates the value of diffusing traffic rather than concentrating it (as identified in Factor#3), as only a small amount of travel at a right-angle to the evacuation can significantly increase the potential capacity of the evacuation routes.

New Jersey businesses suffered massive inventory loss from Hurricane Sandy flooding

Note: evacuation by highway is subject to many variables including unforeseen traffic volume, criminal activity (such as car-jacking, sabotage of traffic signals, obstruction of roadways), traffic accidents (with or without fire), emergency activity (Medevac helicopter or fire engine activity), and/or chemical spills. The key to successful evacuation is to leave early before the mass of persons decide to exit the threatened area.

CHAPTER 7.

MOVING YOUR FAMILY FROM THE DANGER AREA TO SAFETY

Status: You have assembled at the rally point, selected your destination, contacted your host-to-be, settled on the route of travel, loaded the vehicle, and begun the actual movement phase.

Don't speed even if you are afraid. An accident is much more likely if your speed is excessive. If you must stop for some reason, be very careful to park so you cannot be easily blocked in, and do not leave the vehicle unattended at any time.

Listening to the radio may be helpful, but don't be too sure that the information you are hearing is complete or correct. Check different sources if possible and compare what you are hearing. Most often news organizations simply repeat what they are being told by governmental agencies.

Note: Use the CB or HAM radio to <u>monitor local information.</u> Do not reveal your location unless it is necessary for some critical reason. Listening is much more informative than talking.

Remember that everything you say over the radio can be heard by anyone who has the right equipment and is listening.

Beware of persons attempting to stop you on the highway. Do not speed, because that allows less time for you to make decisions when conditions change or trouble may lie ahead.

What if the worst happens during the journey (death, severe injury, separation from loved ones)?

- **Death:** If the situation demands, you may be forced to leave your loved one's remains and push on to your destination.

- **Severe injury:** your family's movement could be delayed for a very long time in this case. Remember that a complete and satisfactory resolution of the injury or illness might not be possible. It might be necessary for you to get what treatment is available and push on to your destination. Medical help <u>might</u> be more available once you leave the immediate danger zone.

- **Separation:** Don't allow this to happen as it could become your worst nightmare. Keep your group in <u>close visual contact</u>, and remember that normal rules ("don't worry dad, I'm just going around the corner and I'll be right back") do not apply. **Separation could be the catastrophe that destroys the whole family.** Stop right where you are until the separated member is located and recovered.

- **You may need help** finding a lost family member, so start asking for local authorities for help immediately. If no authorities are available you will have to improvise. **Don't get into this situation!**

- **Carry recent hard copy pictures** of the family, and <u>close ups of each member with enough facial detail to allow easy identification.</u>

- **Each family member wears a family communications/ID card** (around neck inside clothing). Print and encase in plastic (even a zip-lock bag provides sufficient protection for a 3X5 card). Thus, even if they are not conscious, they can be identified. It is important to have the important phone numbers written down on this card. Having numbers stored in the cell phone may not do any good if the cell phone is not working.

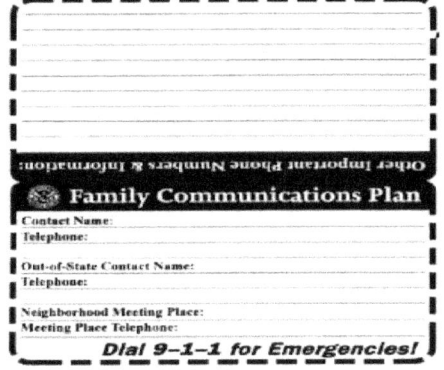

65

- **Car breakdown** (keep your automobiles in good running condition, carry extra oil, replacement belt(s), water, duct tape to temporarily repair radiator hose leaks, brake, and power steering fluid). If you break down en route and cannot continue, you are in real trouble. **You don't want to be leaving the family alone with a broken down car while you go for (what you hope will be) help.**

- **Car-jacking, criminal assault,** common sense protection measures (visually check the area before you stop and park your vehicle). Do not park in a manner that requires backing up if you want to leave in a hurry. Most importantly, if something looks out of order at the location you are considering, just keep moving. Be particularly cautions about allowing children or women to move away from the vehicle where they cannot be protected.

  If the primary route is not passable (road washed out, blocked by authorities etc.): you must have a **paper atlas** or map so you can consider alternatives. Remember that GPS is only useful if the satellites are in good order, no other electronic interference is present, and the programming is complete. You should not trust your GPS to properly represent spatial relationships like a map. Have a hard copy map in case the GPS malfunctions. A regional or national road atlas is not expensive and will be valid for years even though minor details may change.

  If you learn that your original destination is no longer going to receive you, divert to somewhere else. This presents a serious problem. That is why you need to carry address and contact information of any possible alternates. Knowing where you are going, how far it is, and who is waiting for you reduces fear considerably.

SECURITY ISSUES: Stay out of threatening situations. You cannot "win" a fight while your family is exposed and also being threatened. Escape is almost always a better option than battle when your family is present. Always have an escape plan and a last resort defense plan in case escape is blocked. This "unpleasant" contingency must be discussed with the family so everyone understands the basic plan. Don't count on police to rescue you. They may be occupied with other problems and severely under staffed.

HISTORICAL NOTES ON EVACUATION BY AUTOMOBILE

The Houston Texas example (taken from post disaster assessment by the Houston EMA): Common problems during evacuations:

All of the following are observations about the failures of mass evacuations by automobile, based especially on the well-documented evacuation of Houston, which occurred with considerable advance notice of the threat from **Hurricane Rita. It is assumed that future evacuations of major American cities will also be performed primarily by automobile.**

Factor #1: The Bullwhip Effect: The 100-mile traffic jam on the roads extending north from Houston was inevitable, due to the bullwhip effect. As a chain of cars accelerates and decelerates, the longer the chain the greater the change in velocity at the end of the chain. This is due to the same effect as the cracking of a bullwhip; while the end near the user's wrist may only speed up and slow down a little, the opposite tip is moved through the speed of sound (thus creating the trademark "crack" of the whip).

Future evacuations could resolve this problem through the use of pace cars and rolling roadblocks throughout the evacuation path. These pace cars could help reduce the impact of sudden changes in velocity by building a smoother flow of traffic, rather than allowing the buildup of a conventional urban traffic jam.

Factor #2: The Chute: Very much related to the bullwhip effect is the problem of removing people from the evacuation as it is completed. The 100-mile traffic jam was created as virtually everyone in the evacuation line tried to get from Houston to Dallas. The problem is that this <u>extreme concentration of destination</u> meant that any problems absorbing the extra traffic north of Houston were felt all the way back through the evacuation line...creating repercussions throughout the 100-mile line. On the way to Dallas, traffic evacuating Houston via Interstate 45 passed through Huntsville

Future evacuations need to "overshoot" the target destination. Instead of sending people to Dallas, the evacuation should have sent them beyond Dallas, and then absorb them back into the city. The same principle is in effect at any 5k or 10k road race or cross-country run. Runners don't stop moving once they cross the finish line; they move through the "chute", which is a long lane that absorbs them in an orderly manner well past the actual destination of the finish line. The chute allows large numbers of runners to cross the finish line almost simultaneously without landing on top of one another or backing up just a few meters from the finish line. **What any mass evacuation needs is a "chute" of its own -- a method of absorbing the inbound evacuees at a high rate without congesting the evacuation lanes.**

Factor #3: Concentration Instead of Diffusion Northward routes out of Houston: The identified evacuation routes for Houston all points north. While the logical destinations in the event of a hurricane certainly are to the north of the city, that doesn't mean the smart way to get there is by pointing all evacuees in the same direction. This is a lesson that the computer industry knows well; the Internet isn't designed to send all data in the same geographic direction, but instead spreads out the data packets at first, and then lets them re-aggregate once they reach the destination. The same principle is behind Oracle's claim that their grid server "never breaks": Instead of relying on single one-way flow of information, the array of servers adapts to handle computing requirements by distributing the load in many different directions.

Future evacuations need to first disperse all of the people, then let them find their way to the destination. The Houston evacuation routes instead created a massive set of northbound bottlenecks, leaving traffic flowing at ridiculous paces as slow as just one or two miles per hour. Instead, Houstonians should have been scattered in all available directions at first -- northeast, north, northwest, west, and southwest -- then directed northward. Other mass evacuations must do the same whenever possible -- diffusing the people out before their concentration threatens the evacuation itself. **Even an extra hour or two of travel in a direction other than north could have moved lots of people out of the city faster.**

Factor #4: Dependence on Multi-Lane Roads In response to the Houston evacuation, many people will call for more and wider express highway routes out of the city. Yet Houston is already one of the most highway-heavy cities in the country. An increased dependence on a small number of arterial evacuation routes won't make future evacuations better. Part of the trouble with multi-lane expressways is that they limit the number of available alternatives when something goes wrong. Many of the vehicles leaving Houston ran out of gas, and any vehicle that becomes an obstruction makes for serious trouble on a controlled-access roadway like an Interstate highway.

Future evacuations must use smaller highways and two-lane roads as primary modes of evacuation, just as much as they employ expressways. The worst backup that ever emerges on a two-lane road is caused by a slow-moving vehicle, like a tractor. But on a two-lane highway, a tractor can pull over to the side of the road or onto a secondary road, even if only temporarily, in order to let the other vehicles pass. By comparison, a stranded vehicle on an expressway creates a choke point. A well-organized evacuation must include the use of all roads out of a city, including secondary highways and smaller-capacity roads. A two-lane highway can have its opposing lane temporarily reversed and serve about as much traffic as a conventional two-lane expressway -- but only if the authorities are innovative enough to apply such a practice. An investment in better secondary highways (possibly including timed stoplights or better on-the-scene police guidance) would probably be much more efficient and effective at improving emergency evacuations than simply adding more lanes to existing arterial routes.

Illustration: Using Secondary Highways As Evacuation Routes

Evacuation by freeway alone:
Suppose the city of Des Moines, IA was evacuated, with a destination of Omaha, NE. Interstate 80 is a four-lane expressway linking the two cities. But concentrating the entire evacuation on I-80 would inevitably lead to the kind of congestion (grid lock) experienced in Houston.

Evacuation by multiple highways:
Clearly, the use of alternative routes, including the many two-lane highways running east-west between Des Moines and Omaha significantly increases the potential volume of traffic that could be moved out of the city. If even a few two-lane highways were used, they could rapidly equal the capacity of the Interstate route and temporary lane reversal could increase this capacity even more. This further illustrates the value of diffusing traffic rather than concentrating it (as identified in Factor#3), as only a small amount of travel at a right-angle to the evacuation can significantly increase the potential capacity of the evacuation routes.

Cedar Rapids, Iowa, July 4, 2008 -- The railroad attempted to prevent this bridge from being pulled off it's pilings by weighing it down with train cars filled with gravel. In the face of the river's strength during the flood, the attempt was futile. (Susie Shapira/FEMA)

CHAPTER 8.

PRACTICAL FAMILY COMMUNICATIONS

Keeping the family safe and staying current on local information requires communications.

Family communication:

Cell phones may or may not be operational during times of crisis. They may shut down by sheer volume or by government intervention.

The best communication options are HAM radios (range up to 10-20 miles (simplex) depending on conditions, GMRS https://mygmrs.com**), or FRS: walkie-talkie radios. Explanation of each of these options will be discussed in this chapter.**

Need for Communications: Communication is a critical part of any evacuation scenario. Not only is it critical to have communication between family members to coordinate the evacuation, it is essential to safety and emotional well-being to know where everyone is and how they are doing. Without effective communication, family members may be unable to assemble or travel in safety. **Becoming separated in chaotic or threatening situations is not an acceptable option; therefore, communication is most critical.**

Consider CB, GMRS, FRS and/or HAM radio to keep in touch <u>during travel.</u> Cell phones may or may not be usable due to tower damage or overload by many people trying to use them all at once. **Do not rely entirely on cell phones.**

IMPORTANT NOTE: Practice using radios effectively **BEFORE** the emergency. Two-way radio operation is not like using a telephone and

requires practice. Otherwise, it will be very frustrating! <u>Remember that everything you say on the air can be heard by anyone who wants to listen</u>. Be careful what you say!

ASPECTS OF COMMUNICATIONS

- **BETWEEN FAMILY MEMBERS:** Family members must be in communication with each other during evacuation. Staying in close physical proximity is the best solution. Low power radios may also be helpful in some situations.

- **BETWEEN FAMILY AND OTHERS DURING TRAVEL:** It is also a good thing for the family in transit to be communicating with the surrounding area. Situational awareness is critical during these times.

CB RADIO:

The ease and low cost of CB (Citizens Band) mobile communications make this medium very attractive. There is no licensing requirement for the use of CB's, making them available for any "citizen" wishing to talk on them. *It is a very effective but also very non-secure means of short range communication.* With sophisticated antennas the range can be expanded for some distance. When conditions are right, "skip" can be experienced where the signal is sent great distances by bouncing off the ionosphere. However, this is an intermittent phenomenon and is not a reliable means for long range communications. The CB radio has limited channel capacity and available channels will rapidly become overloaded in times of crises. Expect no more than a few miles of effective range depending on terrain.

CELL PHONES:

Beware! Cell phones can be rendered ineffective by a variety of factors. For example, in New York, following the 9-11 attacks, intense cell phone traffic brought the communications system down, and those devices were thus unusable. Cell phone systems have limited capacity for traffic. "All circuits are busy. Please try your call later" can be heard during a normal day! Also be aware that in most localities, cell phone towers begin to shed parts when sustained winds reach around 80 mph (hurricanes, tornadoes). If telephone, land or microwave transmission is interrupted, cell service will also go down. It is important to have the important phone numbers written down on paper and carried with you. Having numbers stored in the cell phone may not do any good if the cell phone is not working.

LAND TELEPHONE LINES:

Fewer and fewer land lines are being used. Many residences have eliminated stationary home phones altogether for the ease and portability of the cell phone. As a result, this transmission capacity is being reduced in order to divert resources to cell service. The reduced capacity of land lines may result in being unable to handle call demand. The caller may hear: "All circuits are busy. Please try your call later". Pay phones are rare.

EXAMPLE: Motorola Talkabout MR350R

FRS: "**Family Radio Service**" or "**walkie –talkies**" are those you will see in parks, playgrounds and amusement parks. They are a very effective and reliable means of communications for parents to keep up with their kids or other groups. They are cheap and effective. However, they cannot be expected to operate beyond their purpose: very short range. Traditionally, they are considered "line of sight" radios. If you can see the other person, you can communicate with them. The range is usually between one half to one mile (despite whatever other claims are made) in a wooded or dense urban area, possibly more on open terrain.

The claim of 2-5 miles <u>may</u> be true between two people on adjoining mountain peaks or on a prairie. No license is required for the use of these radios and they can be easily purchased in retail stores almost anywhere. Typically, these little radios transmit with ½ watt of power.

GMRS or "General Mobile Radio Service": these radios use the same spectrum as the FRS radios and too are limited to "line of sight" range. The main differences are that these radios <u>can</u> operate with higher power expanding the area of reception. <u>Also, the antennas can be detached and replaced by more efficient antennas which will provide increased range</u>. Remember that they are still a "short range" instrument. However, these radios are capable of utilizing a "repeater". A repeater is a separate device that receives the incoming signal, amplifies it and retransmits it on another frequency. This would allow one person to transmit on a GMRS radio to the repeater that may be mounted on the top of a building or mountain. The repeater would then retransmit that signal which could be received by another GMRS radio an equal distance away in the opposite direction. In simpler terms, one radio could talk to another radio 40 miles away if the repeater is between them. Terrain features could distort or shorten the "line of sight" signal.

NOTE: Using the GMRS radios and repeaters requires an FCC license. There are several good sites on the web that discuss the process. However, it is fairly informal and no testing is required. GMRS range can be significantly increased using repeaters but other options may provide greater flexibility.

HAM Radio: The term "HAM" has no particular acronymic meaning, but was a nickname given in the early 20th century to amateur radio operators who liked to show off their capability by producing powerful radio interference to commercial radio stations. HAM today is a thriving international community of individuals connected by their love of the hobby. HAM amateur radio is divided into three categories: VHF (2 meters), UHF (70 cm) and HF. The VHF or Very High Frequency and UHF or Ultra High Frequency is used also by police, fire and emergency services for direct communication. This communication medium is "line of sight".

HAM RADIO FACTORS AND LIMITATIONS:

- VHF or UHF HAM radio is generally effective over a distance up to 10-20 miles. Terrain, antenna, and transceiver power has a definite effect on both receiving and transmission. These radios are made in either mobile (vehicle mounted or hand held) or larger base stations. Operators are required to be licensed by the FCC (Federal Communications Commission). Many counties have clubs that provide support for its members for licensing and use of Ham radios.
- VHF and UHF repeaters are widely found across the United States and the world. Repeaters are often placed on high elevation and can cover entire regions. For example, one mobile radio could use a repeater fifty miles away and receive another radio 50 miles away in the opposite direction, making an effective range of 100 miles. Actual range varies with power, weather conditions, elevation, and natural or man- made obstructions.
- Repeaters can only receive and transmit one user at a time. There can be multiple users on the same repeater but as in any radio conversation, one person must be silent while another talks. In a time of crisis, these too will be over-run in traffic. Remember that there are many repeaters in many areas that can handle a lot of traffic, but like cell phones, in a time emergency the use of repeaters would likely not be effective for direct "one-on-one" communications with a loved one. However, this medium can be very effective to receive the flow of current information on "what's going on out there".
- When the same frequency is monitored by many different people, all who are tuned in can hear the same transmission. Individual calls are not necessary.
- Direct contact between HAM stations is known as simplex. This means that one ham operator speaks to another directly on a frequency outside of the "repeater" network. Again, as previously discussed, it is a "line of sight" situation. However, with a well planned VHF/UHF station, one could speak with a similar station many miles away. Simplex also means that when one party is transmitting; the other must listen until the transmission is complete before replying. **This communication is very much <u>unlike</u> <u>telephone</u> and requires practice before the operator can send and receive effectively.**

EXAMPLE: YAESU
VX-8GR
2M/440 5W HT
BUILTIN GPS

The radio in the photo (right) is one commonly known as a "HT" or "handie-talkie" among hams. The real advantage of carrying this type of radio in your "Go-Bag "is that they can be very capable. It can transmit and receive on multiple bands. It can transmit and receive on VHF (2meter), (UHF) 440 (70cm) ham frequencies and also receive commercial FM and AM stations. It addition, it may receive many aviation, public service and NOAA (National Oceanic & Atmospheric Administration) transmissions. This would be very valuable in a time of emergency not only to communicate but to acquire situational awareness in your surroundings. The one shown has a built in GPS. If you ever find yourself "bewildered" regarding your location in the turmoil of an emergency, you can transmit your location with the same radio. These little radios can be a lifesaver. Beware however, they are low powered (5 watts) and have limited range.

HF: HIGH FREQUENCY OR (SHORT WAVE): is the best known medium where persons across the earth can communicate directly. This medium requires a properly configured antenna, radio, and FCC license. Signal strength is dependent on the quality and power of the radio transceiver, and the antennas both at transmitting and receiving site. This signal is bounced off the ground, travels into space, and is bounced back to earth by the ionosphere where it is once again reflected into the upper atmosphere to be once more reflected etc. It is quite common for these signals to circle the earth as they bounce many times. This process allows the operators to conduct one-on-one communications at great distances. Most of the HF sets can be operated on DC (12 volts) current thus making them very portable.

Example Yaesu FT 897D

The radio shown above is one of the most capable ham radios on the market today. It has the capability of transmitting and receiving on **every** amateur band available: VHF,UHF and HF. It can serve as a base station or a mobile unit. It has the capability of an internal battery pack for portable power. It would be very suitable for the communication needs of the shelter and removed in a hurry if the need arises and taken off site or in a vehicle.

Ham radio offers the most communications independence and flexibility during a crisis, even if the operator is only listening to other transmissions.

NOTE: The FCC does require a license for the use of all Ham radios. Most every local area has a Ham radio club that offers testing and there are many effective study sites on the Web. HAMs are licensed at three levels: Technician, General, and Extra. The Technician level will grant all privileges for allotted UHF and VHF spectrum. High frequency (HF) utilization requires at least a General License.

REMINDER: **all civilian radio transmissions can be heard by anyone having a receiver tuned to the appropriate frequency. Be VERY cautious about what information is spoken over the airwaves: there is no way to tell who might be listening.**

Contact a local HAM club to discuss how to study for the required license or go on line to www.arrl.com.

Summary: The FRS radios are cheap and effective. However, they only put out ½ watt and have very short range. The GMRS radios are better as they can generate more power and have "repeater" capability. Hand held Ham radios, usually generate 5 watts and also have "repeater capability". Mobile Ham radio stations typically generate between 50 and 75 watts and have multiple antenna options giving it tremendous power and capability. Mobile HF is very viable but expensive. Base station HF will generate the best long distance communication system anywhere. Another option is to find a surplus commercial or public safety radio that can be programmed to the ham band such as a Motorola Saber. They typically generate 5 watts.

But remember: **"When all else fails… Ham Radio!"**

Radio wave spectrum

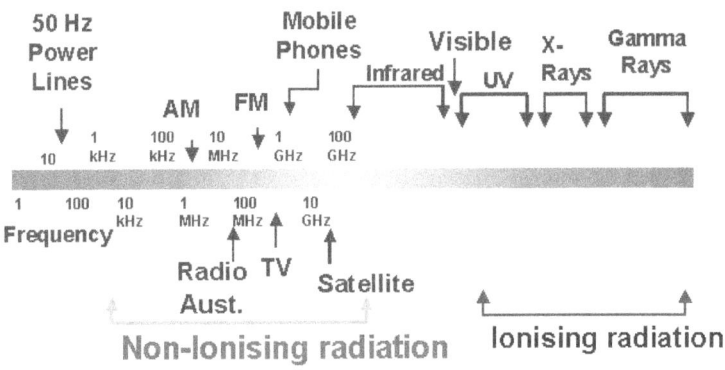

American Radio Relay League

CHAPTER 9.

WHAT TO DO WHEN YOU ARRIVE AT YOUR DESTINATION

Relatives/Close Friends

- **Offer to pay them** – your presence costs them money. Even if they decline, find some way to help support the household. Do everything possible to support yourself.
- **Even if your presence is temporary, <u>get a job</u>** (even a temp job) and buy some groceries or pay the electric bill. Don't ask your hosts if they want you to do this, just do it. Lying around someone else's house while they support you will erode your dignity, depress you and in the long run irritate them. Do not expect them to indefinitely provide for your family <u>and</u> theirs. Counsel formally with the head of the house as to your intentions and keep them advised of your progress. **Respect the sacrifices they are making to help you.**
- **Moving in with relatives is highly stressful for everyone**, even if you are related to these good people. The first few nights are like a camp out, but that gets old in a hurry.
- **<u>Cheerfully</u> observe your host's schedule** (if they retire early to sleep, do the same – don't stay up late and disrupt their sleep. Remember, they are going to work next morning while you get to sleep in.
- They are feeding you, do the dishes and clean house. **Show gratitude by your attitude and helpful actions.**
- **After you offer to pay them something, then just give it to them.** Don't embarrass them with a long conversation. If they really want to be generous they can save all the money and give it back to you as you go back home.

- **No matter how generous your hosts are, <u>it is NOT your house</u>, and <u>you are a guest.</u>** Behave respectfully, take a good share of the daily chores, and help without being asked. Take out the garbage, rake the yard, walk the dog, or whatever is of value to them.
- **If you bring a pet, your host's irritation factor may go up rapidly.** Your cute little Maltese may not like your host's cat. **A problem between pets could well cause your family to be asked to leave,** or at least create serious stress in your relationship. If you hope to stay for an extended period, adapt to your host's life and way of doing things. Bring pet supplies with you, and figure a way to take care of your pet without displacing theirs. They may not allow pets in the house. Find a way to work with that. **It's YOUR problem, not your host's.**
- **Have an alternate plan in case they ask you to leave.**
- **You are a guest (even if you are family), so make yourself useful.**
- Make it a priority to fit into your hosts' home life with minimum disruption of their routine. Volunteer to help with household chores and do extra things to demonstrate your gratitude. Your host is making a sacrifice by allowing you to stay under his roof.
- Establish a practical away-from-home living pattern that includes employment, maintaining physical health, and spiritual/emotional strength. Attend church together, respect your host and their schedule, try to add value to your host by your presence.
- If conditions improve and return to home becomes possible, your plan includes organizing that movement.
- If return to your home is not possible, your plan includes how you might reestablish home and employment.

Compassionate Acquaintances

- Offer to pay them— your presence costs them money. Even if they decline, find some way to help support the household.
- Your host may become your best friends <u>or</u> the experience may quickly turn sour. Adapting to another family sharing the same home is difficult. Don't underestimate the magnitude of disruption your family will cause. Have an alternate plan in case they ask you to leave.
- Do everything you can to help out and minimize the disruption caused by your presence.

- The other rules are the same as above, except be hard at work on a plan to get your family under its own roof. Unless you are very fortunate, this compassion may be relatively short lived.

Hotel/Motel

- Park your vehicle where you can keep an eye on it, don't leave family members alone in the room even for a short period, secure your credit and ID information carefully. These factors sound simple but may be difficult in practice. Remember that general public behavior may be altered by the excitement and fear inherent in evacuation.
- Unload as much as you can from your automobile and bring it into the room. **Nothing left in an automobile is secure.**

Employment (now and later)

Find a job as soon as possible after you arrive!

- If you have followed the advice on packing, you will have one set of interview clothing, resume, and references. As the evacuation continues, and other displaced persons move in, jobs will dry up completely and wages will be depressed. A part-time job sweeping floors might be a good deal if it connects you to the locals and helps keep your family alive. Your hosts are more likely to remain compassionate if you are contributing to your upkeep, however little that may be.
- If you cannot get a job immediately, <u>volunteer your talents and services</u> (for example) at the hospital or local municipality. You need to meet people who can help you, and that is one of the best ways to do so.
- Resume and references with phone numbers and complete contact information (keep your resume in both hard copy – paper and on electronic media. Save the electronic copies in earlier versions of popular software so they can more probably be read even by older computers should those be the only ones available) wherever you may call home.
- If possible stay in touch with former employers and references even if they also must evacuate. Opportunities may develop later and a network is still very important.

- Copies of your basic ID including social security card (never surrender the actual card except to civil authorities or if required for copying at actual time of employment), driver's license, professional certifications (medical license, nursing license etc).

Frank Loftus/The HSUS Pet evacuation, and reuniting with families – photo courtesy of FEMA

CHAPTER 10.

SHELTER IN PLACE, RETURNING, SCAVENGING

Shelter in place: Successful sheltering in place requires an uncommon mentality.

- Assume no stores are open, and the only opportunity for goods from the "outside" is what you can trade with the neighbors. Therefore, what do you have to trade?
- Roof damage from various storms can make living in your damaged house miserable, Buy two or three plastic tarps and store them in an convenient location. You will also need a box of large, square-headed roofing nails.
- Light-weight painting drop-cloth plastic makes a useful temporary cover for broken windows. Have a heavy duty staple gun with a box of 1/2" staples in your inventory. Garbage bags can also be split and used to cover broken windows.
- Two rolls of duct tape will prove very useful.
- Lack of fuel may become a serious problem. Make a habit of NEVER allowing your automobile tank to drop below 1/2 tank. You may be able to siphon or drain a few gallons from the lawn mower, and other small engines. Be careful NOT to cross-contaminate 2 cycle mixed with unmixed gas.
- LP has no storage life limit, and may be kept in different sized cylinders. This makes an excellent choice for back up cooking and some forms of heaters (beware carbon monoxide risk).

Food and basic necessities

- Reorganize your food inventory into the following categories immediately if you are going to stay in your home. Each category will be handled differently.
  - Dry staples requiring cooking
  - Food items not requiring cooking
  - Frozen/refrigerated items: refrigeration (residual cold) may last 24 hours if the refrigerator/freezer is left completely undisturbed. What will you do with the refrigerator/freezer contents? Cooking meats and other frozen items on the backyard grill is one possibility, but then how will you store the cooked items so they will not quickly spoil? Depending on the situation, salting meat may be an option, but that is a skill that you must acquire <u>before</u> the emergency occurs. If you keep a large amount of food in your freezer much of it will likely be wasted.
  - Snacks (control these carefully or they will be eaten too quickly).
  - Garden items (if you have a garden)
- Hygiene is critical to health. How will you bathe and wash clothing? A large bucket or tub will be very useful for washing clothing and persons. A <u>clean</u> toilet plunger can help with clothes washing.
- It would be wise to maintain a significant supply (minimum of six months) of staple food items (beans, rice, pasta etc.) in an easily stored form (cans or Mylar pouches).
- Water is critical to survival, but even in a disaster pressure remains for a time in the water lines. Make a plan to fill specific containers for drinking and other uses. You will need to access these containers quickly in the event of impending trouble, so store them accordingly.
- Potable water remains in toilet flush tanks, and water heaters. Make a plan as to how you will remove this water and for what purposes you will use it. Rationing will be necessary, with primary attention to personal hydration.

Returning, Scavenging:

What has real value after widespread devastation?

The issue of remaining property value may or may not be relevant. Consider what are known as basic human needs. If your home, even though damaged can still provide decent shelter and some food/clothing/supplies, staying nearby might be much better than the nearest high school gymnasium with five hundred other displaced persons. Items that have basic value will be important (e.g. tools, food, clothing, household effects such as pots, pans, dishes, cups, cleaning supplies, nails, buckets, toilet paper). Personal items like jewelry, electronics or expensive clothing may or may not have significant value. Remember the post WWII German civilians who traded their most prized possessions to farmers for food. In 1946 many a pig reclined on a rug that once graced a well-to-do living room. **Stick to basics and don't be distracted trying to salvage all the "extras".**

If you scavenge or recover items, what are you going to do with them?

- **Sell or barter** (consider needs for your own family's likely consumption or use; how long you think it will be before supplies are once again available on the open market). Plan to share with your neighbors, and work together to endure or mitigate the effects of inevitable shortages. Money may or may not have relevant value depending on the scope, nature, and duration of the problem, so don't count on currency to solve every supply problem. Successful barter is a talent. Compare it to living in yard-sale world every day.

- **Use for your immediate needs:** don't expect your life to go on as it had before the disaster. Make a family project out of cutting back and improvising. Share ideas with your neighbors. Look for success, find a way to laugh about shortages or failures. Stay loose and remember that you can reshape your part of the world more than you may imagine.

- **Share supplies with others who are also in need:** <u>voluntary</u> sharing knits families and communities together. Following a disaster, unity of purpose is the most vital commodity. Keep this activity simple, and don't fall into the trap of stockpiling everything in one place (it will have to be guarded, and disbursed, thus opening the door to many abuses).

- **The concept of private property (still a constitutional right) does not disappear just because a disaster has occurred.** The quickest way to start serious trouble is to attempt to confiscate the property of others through actions of an ad-hoc "democratic" citizens' committee. Share because it is the right thing, or announce your intentions not to do so. Remember that if you decline to share you will find others less inclined to assist you.

Perhaps you can stay at (if not inside) your damaged home. This approach helps in many ways. You know neighbors and can assist/share with them; you can salvage items from your home, and protect your property

See our companion book "Surviving Disaster Without Leaving Home" for an in depth examination of this contingency.

Alaska earthquake road damage – FEMA photo

CHAPTER 11.

STARTING A NEW LIFE

Millions of people have been displaced by war, famine, and other natural disasters. It <u>CAN</u> happen, but you can start over if necessary.

Fit in with your hosts and be useful: The primary element that will help your family successfully live in another household is respect for your benefactors.

Serve your new community: Volunteer as soon as possible in your new community. Use all of your skills to benefit your host family and neighbors. Build a positive reputation as rapidly as possible. Don't expect immediate acceptance, but be patient as you work to establish your value to your new community.

Hold your family together: Enroll children in the new school, meet the teachers and school administration. Volunteer for fund raisers, work parties, and school cultural events. Bring your talents and share them freely (but don't start telling them how you did it back home – that is usually irritating). Bring ideas up generically, not attached to your former area of residence.

Maintain your faith: Join a church, and help out. It has long been recognized that faith in God strengthens individuals and families. Forced displacement into an unfamiliar area opens an opportunity to renew faith and family solidarity.

Maintain your core values: Spend time together as a family and support one another as each one seeks new direction for life. All family members will be stressed by displacement, not just the primary bread winner. Make a special time each week to gather the family and review the situation. Emphasize gratitude for any good thing, no matter how small it may appear. Sing together, pray together, play a game together, and listen as each member shares what may be in their heart.

Get a job in your new location: Meet people in the community and ask them for help to get to know everyone. Among your new neighbors you will find some of great compassion and generosity who will help you move forward. When anyone blesses your family with a gift or support of any kind, make it a point to do something for them no matter how small it may seem or how much they may protest that they don't have any needs. Honest reciprocation of generosity will build a good reputation more quickly than any other behavior. Demonstrate your thanks by doing something good.

Hoboken N.J. transit station controls were destroyed by Hurricane Sandy flooding – FEMA photo

Chapter 12.

<u>PETS</u>

If you have pets, plan to care for them no matter what. It is grossly irresponsible and cruel to abandon pets to starvation or expect them to be fed and cared for by someone else in a refugee area. If you have pets, leaving will require more time. If you leave early and are wrong (the storm turns another direction), no harm has been done.

Large animals such as horses present special problems including feeding, shelter, and transportation that may hinder human evacuation. These must be carefully considered and accommodated in your planning process.

Assemble a small pet care kit with the following components. This should fit in one portable container.

- Orange plastic safety fence. This works well for most dogs, and usually comes in 100' rolls (photo). An effective temporary containment fence can be constructed using ten 36" wooden stakes and zip ties.
- Dry food for <u>at least two weeks</u>, medication as necessary
- Food and water feeding dishes and 2 gallon water storage container (collapsible)
- Cats or other small animals will require crates/cages since they are not easily contained by fencing
- 8' X 8' tarp with nylon cord sufficient to make an overhead shelter or lean-to
- Ten plastic tent stakes (and hammer) to reinforce stakes or secure plastic fencing if necessary (at ground level)

- It is understood that pets often become like children within a family, however their presence must never be allowed to jeopardize family safety. Plan ahead or be prepared for serious trouble with your animals.

HUMANE SOCIETY OF THE UNITED STATES LINKS

http://www.humanesociety.org/Disaster preparedness for pets The Humane Society of the United States

The key to survival during a disaster, crisis or emergency is to be as prepared as possible before the storm hits. Take the time to make a plan and assemble an emergency kit for you and your pet. By taking these steps now, you will greatly increase your pet's chances of survival.

Prepare for everyday emergencies

These are examples of what could happen to you at anytime, anywhere in the country. Prepare yourself for these events, and if a large disaster should ever hit, you will be ready and know what to do:

- The roads are icy, traffic is a mess and you decide to stay with a friend instead of risking the drive home from school or work. Who will check on your cat and feed her?
- While you were out running errands, a propane truck overturned on the street near your neighborhood and you are not allowed to go home. A police officer tells you the electricity to your neighborhood was shut off. How can you make sure your birds stay warm?
- Your mother-in-law has had a heart attack and you are going to meet your wife at the hospital. It may be a long night. Who will give your dog his medicine?

The Humane Society of the United States recommends the following actions to make sure your pets are taken care of when everyday events like these prevent you from taking care of your pets:

- Find a trusted neighbor and give them a key to your house or barn. Make sure this person is comfortable and familiar with your pets.

- Make sure the neighbor knows your pets' whereabouts and habits, so they will not have to waste precious time trying to find or catch them.
- Create a pet emergency/disaster kit and place it in a prominent place where your neighbor can find it.
- If the emergency involves evacuation, make sure the neighbor would be willing to take your pets and has access to the appropriate carriers and leashes. Plan to meet at a prearranged location.
- If you use a pet sitting service, they may be available to help, but discuss the possibility well in advance.

Disaster supply checklist

Every member of your family should know what he or she needs to take when you evacuate. You also need to prepare supplies for your pet. Stock up on non-perishables well ahead of time, and have everything ready to go at a moment's notice. Keep everything accessible, stored in sturdy containers (duffel bags, covered trash containers, etc.) that can be carried easily.

If you reside in an area prone to certain seasonal disasters, such as flooding or hurricanes that might require evacuation, create a kit to keep in your car. In your pet disaster kit, you should include:

- Food and water for at least five days for each pet, bowls and a manual can opener if you are packing canned pet food.
- Medications and medical records stored in a waterproof container and a first aid kit. A pet first aid book is also good to include.
- Cat litter box, litter, garbage bags to collect all pets' waste, and litter scoop.
- Sturdy leashes, harnesses, and carriers to transport pets safely and to ensure that your pets can't escape. Carriers should be large enough for the animal to stand comfortably, turn around and lie down. Your pet may have to stay in the carrier for hours at a time while you are away from home. These may require blankets or towels for bedding and warmth, and other special items.
- Current photos and descriptions of your pets to help others identify them in case you and your pets become separated and to prove that they are yours.
- Pet beds and toys, if you can easily take them, to reduce stress.

- Information about your pets' feeding schedules, medical conditions, behavior problems, and the name and number of your veterinarian in case you have to board your pets or place them in foster care.

Other useful items include newspapers, paper towels, plastic trash bags, grooming items and household bleach.

Settle on a safe destination before the emergency occurs

Because evacuation shelters generally don't accept pets (except for service animals), you must plan ahead to make certain your family and pets will have a safe place to stay. Don't wait until disaster strikes to do your research.

- Contact hotels and motels outside your immediate area to check policies on accepting pets. Ask about any restrictions on number, size and species. Inquire if the "no pet" policies would be waived in an emergency. Make a list of animal-friendly places and keep it handy. Call ahead for a reservation as soon as you think you might have to leave your home.
- Check with friends, relatives or others outside your immediate area. Ask if they would be able to shelter you and your animals or just your animals, if necessary. If you have more than one pet, you may need to house them at separate locations.
- Make a list of boarding facilities and veterinary offices that might be able to shelter animals in emergencies; include 24-hour telephone numbers. Ask your local animal shelter if it provides foster care or shelter for pets in an emergency. This should be your last resort, as shelters have limited resources and are likely to be stretched to their limits during an emergency.

In case you're not home when trouble comes

An evacuation order may come, or a disaster may strike, when you're at work or out of the house.

- Make arrangements well in advance for a trusted neighbor to take your pets and meet you at a specified location. Be sure the person is comfortable with your pets and your pets are familiar with him/her, knows where your animals are likely to be, knows where your disaster supplies are kept and has a key to your home.

Don't forget ID

Your pet should be wearing up-to-date identification at all times. This includes adding your current cell phone number to your pet's tag. It may also be a good idea to include the phone number of a friend or relative outside your immediate area, if your pet is lost, you'll want to provide a number on the tag that will be answered even if you're out of your home.

One tree devastates New Jersey house – FEMA photo

When you evacuate, take your pets

• The single most important thing you can do to protect your pets is to take them with you when you evacuate.

- Animals left behind in a disaster can easily be injured, lost or killed. Animals left inside your home can escape through storm-damaged areas, such as broken windows, or be trapped and burn or drown.

- Animals turned loose to fend for themselves are likely to become victims of exposure, starvation, predators, contaminated food or water, or accidents. Leaving dogs tied or chained outside in a disaster is a death sentence.

- If you leave, even if you think you may only be gone for a few hours, take your animals. When you leave, you have no way of knowing how long you'll be kept out of the area, and you may not be able to go back for your pets.

- Leave early; don't wait for a mandatory evacuation order. An unnecessary trip is far better than waiting too long to leave safely with your pets. If you wait to be evacuated by emergency officials, you may be told to leave your pets behind.

If you don't evacuate, shelter in place

- If your family and pets must wait out a storm or other disaster at home, identify a safe area of your home where you can all stay together. Be sure to close your windows and doors, stay inside, and follow the instructions from your local emergency management office.
- Bring your pets indoors as soon as local authorities say there is an imminent problem. Keep pets under your direct control; if you have to evacuate, you will not have to spend time trying to find them. Keep dogs on leashes and cats in carriers, and make sure they are wearing identification.
- If you have a room you can designate as a "safe room," put your emergency supplies in that room in advance, including your pet's crate and supplies. Have any medications and a supply of pet food and water inside watertight containers, along with your other emergency supplies. If there is an open fireplace, vent, pet door, or similar opening in the house, close it off with plastic sheeting and strong tape.
- Listen to the radio periodically, and don't come out until you know it's safe.

After the storm

Planning and preparation will help you survive the disaster, but your home may be a very different place afterward, whether you have taken shelter at home or elsewhere.

- Don't allow your pets to roam loose. Familiar landmarks and smells might be gone, and your pet will probably be disoriented. Pets can easily get lost in such situations.
- While you assess the damage, keep dogs on leashes and keep cats in carriers inside the house. If your house is damaged, they could escape and become lost.
- Be patient with your pets after a disaster. Try to get them back into their normal routines as soon as possible, and be ready for behavioral problems that may result from the stress of the situation. If behavioral problems persist, or if your pet seems to be having any health problems, talk to your veterinarian.

Find out in advance where you can take your pets when an emergency happens in your community.

Jersey city, N.J. roadway undercut by Hurricane Sandy flood waters – FEMA photo

CHAPTER 13.

WHAT IF YOU ARE THE HOST AND HAVE ELECTED TO SHELTER DISPLACED PERSONS?

You and your guests will think the new arrangements are like a camp out for about 48 hours. Then the feeling of relief will be replaced by all the practical problems associated with two (or more) families living where one resided before. Here are a few practical guidelines to consider:

Under these conditions it is important to understand that EVERYONE will be under increased stress.

- Set rules of the house. It's your place, so that's perfectly reasonable. Just be sure that when you set rules, you follow them yourself. Everyone's nerves will be tested as they adjust, so keep things fair and reasonable.

- Carve out some space for the guests to occupy, manage, and care for. This will help them to get organized and maintain some accountability for their possessions.

- Understand that they will not keep house exactly the way you do. Tell them of your expectations up front.

- Schedule time for them to use the washer, dryer, and other appliances. Make a note on a calendar so everyone will recall the conversation.

- Establish a lights out time. A TV-off time might be necessary as well. Children will require the patience of all.

- Discuss how you will work food preparation and consumption. Going to the refrigerator for a snack may not work like it used to.

- Don't allow misunderstandings to fester, but cultivate respect and patience. Help the breadwinner to maintain self respect by asking them to do chores, even if they do them a little differently than you. Be flexible in this regard, and listen to their suggestions as to how to make things work.

- Discuss financial concerns frankly with the adults, and work together to mitigate the strains on everyone.

- Introduce your guests to others in the community so they can make friends. Recommend them or let them know that you will not do so.

This difficult and stressful experience can be uplifting and faith-building or it can degenerate into a deep pool of trouble. You can and should work closely and honestly with your guests so things remain on a reasonable track. Difficulties and adjustments are inevitable but when both parties are honestly trying for a solution, success is almost guaranteed.

f love and true generosity, you will find great fulfillment.

Here is a visual of a typical "emotional rollercoaster" experienced by most victims:

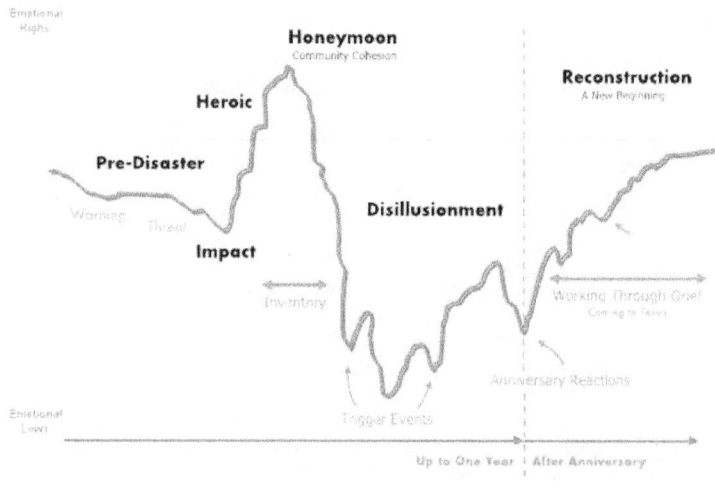

Summary: Expect your guests to pitch in and share with the chores. Outline this in the beginning so they will know they are expected to help. They should help cook, clean and pickup for the group or after themselves if that is what is decided.

The biggest hazard is when the guests feel comfortable with the situation and begin to take advantage of the hosts (or vice versa). Have regular discussions on state of affairs, timetables and adjustments as necessary. Guests who chip in and help are great! Those who don't will become a nuisance very quickly. If you are "hosting" out of town guests for any extended period, do both you and them a favor and agree on some basic rules as well as discuss how things are going for both of you.

Catano, Puerto Rico, October 26, 2009 -- Damages caused to the petroleum tanks. Twenty one out of forty tanks from the refinery were affected by the explosion and subsequent fires. (Yuisa Rios/FEMA photo)

CHAPTER 14.

SUMMARY

SURVIVAL PLANNING RECAP:

- **Become aware of the need for evacuation early** so you can act decisively. Become and remain aware of the status of your surroundings and the development of threats. Don't wait until everyone else tries to leave.

- **Gather your family and loved ones and review plans** in advance of developing chaos. Reassure one another that your mutual efforts will enable you to get through whatever is ahead. Use the checklist found here in this book as a basic to do list. Improve it as necessary to fit your situation.

- **Plan to be able to leave on short notice** with appropriate supplies, documents, and information. Extra fuel can be stored, and supplies pre-packed to smooth departure if necessary. Consider purchasing a small utility trailer to carry supplies and fuel.

- **If at all possible head for a pre-planned destination** where your family can be at least temporarily sheltered by extended family or close friends. Don't imagine that you can just pull off the road at a motel. Thousands of others on the road will have the same thing in mind. Also don't expect that just because you made a reservation, the room will be held. Don't fight if the room has been given to someone else (who offered more money). Move on. Also don't expect the continental breakfast to be served as usual. Many of the guests won't have eaten in 24 hours because they were not prepared.

- **Plan how to deal with possible death or separation** from loved ones. Depending on how severe the situation is, you may not be able to linger if death occurs. Separation or serious injury demands search, retrieval, and/or some medical treatment of the lost member. That distraction may well be very dangerous for the whole family. Don't become separated.

- **Work together to strengthen emotional resilience to minimize uncertainty, fear, and depression.**

- Stick together, pray, sing, and take comfort from mutual support. Reassure one another and help keep the whole family safe. Hold onto and nurture each member of the family emotionally and spiritually, and hold fast to your core values and faith.

- **You will have to carry some cash.** Depending on the nature of the emergency, you may or may not have debit or ATM access. Do not show large amounts of money when paying for gas or food. You do not know who may be targeting you. Also expect the price of basic commodities like food, ice, gasoline to increase exorbitantly. If you aren't willing to pay the high prices, move on and don't argue.

- **Collect and store supplies before you need them.** Don't panic, but work your plan.

- **Expect chaos and that parts of your plan will fail** and must be modified.

- **Long range expectations must be flexible**

THIS PAGE MARKS THE END OF THEORY AND THE BEGINNING OF THE ACTUAL PREPARATIONS:

NOW, LETS GO TO WORK!

Remember: When the time has come to act, the time for preparation has passed!

Action checklist:

1) Assess the likely threats in your area.
2) Discuss with family.
3) Create your action plan and determine a completion date – discuss with all family members as you make progress.
4) Begin to purchase containers and supplies, review maps, and build your sources of local information.
5) Review your plan annually or when local conditions change.

Communications (Chapter 9)

1) Set up time to discuss with spouse

_____

2) Have family council to discuss with children

_____

3) Communicate plan to extended family

_____

4) Communicate plan to possible host

_____

Rally points

1 Primary (nearest)

_____

#2 Secondary (intermediate distance)

_____

#3 Fail Safe (most distant)

_____

Assemble go-bags for each member of family (and pets)
Weight of each pack (no more than 10-20% of total body weight)

1) _____ lbs   for whom _____
2) _____ lbs   for whom _____

3) _____lbs   for whom _____
4) _____lbs   for whom _____
5) _____lbs   for whom _____

Make basic content list for your five portable container system, use suggested contents in text for a template _____/_____

Completion target actual dates for completing each container.

        #1 shelter _____/_____
        #2 food _____/_____
        #3 clothing _____/_____
        #4 personal papers _____/_____
        #5 medical and other support supplies (including provisions for pets if applicable) _____/_____

Assemble and package necessary maps _____/_____

Talk with relatives and friends and determine who would be willing to shelter your family in case evacuation was necessary _____/_____ results

_____

Distribute the written plan to all involved

Schedule dates to review and revise as needed

Share your thoughts and ideas with others who are interested

Evacuation Plan

Name _____

How will we know the plan has been activated? (in case you are
separated) _____

How will the activation of the plan be communicated? _____

What is the **level of Preparation? (pg 30)** _____

Where are the **Rally Points? (pg32):**

       Primary (1): _____

       Secondary (2):_____

       Emergency/Fail safe (3): _____

What is the **departure route? (pg35):** _____

       Alternate Route: _____

Go Bags (pg42):
Which one is assigned to whom?

Person	Which Bag

What is your **ultimate destination? (pg57)**

       Primary (D1) _____

       Secondary (D2): _____

       Emergency/Fail safe: _____

Method of Communications? (pg71)

	Person	How
Mom/Dad		
Kids		
Extended Family		
Possible Host		

<u>Distribute copies to all family members.</u>

You may use this template to point you in the right direction. Adjust and
adapt as needed.

Go-Bag (72 hours) list

Water: pack at least one gallon of water. You will need one gallon each day to avoid debilitating dehydration.

Food: This food is for emergency only.

Clothing: Change into traveling clothes before beginning evacuation if possible, comfortable shoes (sneakers, hikers), already broken in! Two changes of underwear rip stop pants, poncho, three changes of socks, two t-shirts, down or poly filled jacket <u>with</u> waterproof breathable shell, floppy hat with brim, composite (warm) gloves.

Fire starters: Carry all of the following: matches, flint and steel, and a butane lighter.

Flashlight and spare batteries: LED or wind up flash lights

First aid kit: Carry only a small basic first aid package.

Toilet paper: remove the cardboard tube and flatten the roll to save space. Store in a zip lock freezer bag.

Lip balm: You will become dehydrated, and this will help.

Sun screen: SPF 30 It must be used to be effective.

Fishing-line: hooks. In case it takes you longer to travel than you have food.

Parachute cord: 50 ft (15 m).

Duct tape: Store in zip lock bag.

Personal items: Soap, toothbrush, toothpaste, and floss. Personal hygiene (women's hygiene and/or baby care) is essential for survival.

Garbage bags: 2 (30 gal), extra zip lock or poncho.

Sleeping bag: or cold weather pants that can be connected to the jacket.

Compass and topographical map: of every county you'll traverse on the way to your primary or alternate destination.

Pepper spray or other defensive items: use your own best judgment, and remain within legal bounds

Pencil and paper. To leave notes If necessary

Multi-tool and sheath knife

MRE at least one so you don't have to cook one meal (six meals would be better)

Emergency whistle for signaling

Other convenience items: tent **(**dome type is easy to set up in a small area, and may not require lines and tent pegs) one small aluminum pot with lid, utensils, alcohol stove, GPS/compass and GMRS/FRS (2 meter HAM is best) radio transceiver, 8×10 tarp, compact survival plant reference guide, survival knife, military folding entrenching tool or small shovel

Cash: Small bills

FAMILY ID CARD

Make copies and put in zip lock bags or waterproof sheet protector in each person's go bag or on their person, in the unfortunate event you become separated. This is especially important for the children.

Photograph
Date of photograph: _____

_____
Name
_____
Last Address:

Blood type _____ allergies _____
Special medical needs _____

Please contact my parents

Secondary Rally Point

Primary Rally point

_____

_____

Emergency Rally Point:

Names_____

_____

PRIMARY TELEPHONE CONTACT NUMBERS

HOME_____

CELL _____

NEAREST RELATIVES

1) NAME _____

ADDRESS _____

PHONE NUMBERS _____

2) NAME _____

ADDRESS _____

PHONE NUMBERS _____

ALTERNATE CONTACTS

1) Name _____

STREET_____

CITY_____

STATE_____

HOME PHONE_____

CELL _____

2) Name _____

STREET_____

CITY _____

STATE _____

HOME PHONE_____

CELL_____

FIRST AID KIT

Put together an emergency kit (information supplied by the American Red Cross and FEMA)

Are you ready?
While the lessons of Hurricane Katrina are fresh in our minds, it's time to prepare supplies to be ready for a major emergency or natural disaster

If a natural disaster struck in Oregon, would your family be prepared? Earthquakes, floods, wildfires, even tsunamis all have the potential to cause widespread destruction here.

Learn more on Family Disaster Planning from the Red Cross
- Prepare at Home
- Prepare at School
- Prepare at Work
- Prepare in your Community

In putting an emergency or disaster kit together, there are six basics you should stock for your home: water, food, first aid supplies, clothing and bedding, tools and emergency supplies, and special items. If you have camping gear, you're already on your way to having an emergency kit.

Also remember you don't have to put your kit together in one day. Set a timetable to have a complete kit over a 3 - 6 month period to lessen the onetime cost and hassle of trying to gather everything at once.

Keep the items that you would most likely need during an evacuation in an easy-to carry container--suggested items are marked with an asterisk (*) noted below in list.

Possible containers for a home kit include a large, covered trash container, a camping backpack, or a duffel bag.

For a portable kit, use a day pack or duffel with shoulder strap. Keep an extra kit in your car.

Water
*Store water in plastic containers such as soft drink bottles. Avoid using containers that will decompose or break, such as milk cartons or glass

bottles. A normally active person needs to drink at least two quarts of water each day. Hot environments and intense physical activity can double that amount. Children, nursing mothers, and ill people will need more.

* Store one gallon of water per person per day.

* Keep at least a three-day supply of water per person (two quarts for drinking, two quarts for each person in your household for food preparation/sanitation).*

Food
* Store at least a three-day supply of non-perishable food. Select foods that require no refrigeration, preparation or cooking, and little or no water. If you must heat food, pack a can of sterno. Select food items that are compact and lightweight. Include a selection of the following foods in your Disaster Supplies Kit:

* Ready-to-eat canned meats, fruits, and vegetables
* Canned juices
* Staples (salt, sugar, pepper, spices, etc.)
* High energy foods
* Vitamins
* Food for infants
* Comfort/stress foods

First Aid Kit
Assemble a first aid kit for your home and one for each car.

* Sterile adhesive bandages in assorted sizes
* Assorted sizes of safety pins
* Cleansing agent/soap
* Latex gloves (2 pairs)
* Sunscreen
* 2-inch sterile gauze pads (4-6)
* 4-inch sterile gauze pads (4-6)
* Triangular bandages (3)
* Non-prescription drugs
* 2-inch sterile roller bandages (3 rolls)
* 3-inch sterile roller bandages (3 rolls)
* Scissors
* Tweezers
* Needle

* Moistened towelettes
* Antiseptic
* Thermometer
* Tongue blades (2)
* Tube of petroleum jelly or other lubricant

Non-Prescription Drugs
* Aspirin or non aspirin pain reliever
* Anti-diarrhea medication
* Antacid (for stomach upset)
* Syrup of Ipecac (use to induce vomiting if advised by the Poison Control Center)
* Laxative
* Activated charcoal (use if advised by the Poison Control Center)

Tools and Supplies
* Mess kits, or paper cups, plates, and plastic utensils*
* Emergency preparedness manual*
* Battery-operated radio and extra batteries*
* Flashlight and extra batteries*
* Cash or traveler's checks, change*
* Non-electric can opener, utility knife*
* Fire extinguisher: small canister ABC type
* Tube tent or camping/backpack tent
* Pliers
* Tape
* Compass
* Matches in a waterproof container
* Aluminum foil
* Plastic storage containers
* Signal flare
* Paper, pencil
* Needles, thread
* Medicine dropper
* Shut-off wrench, to turn off household gas and water
* Whistle
* Plastic sheeting
* Map of the area (for locating shelters)

Sanitation
 Toilet paper, "towelettes"
* Soap, liquid detergent*
* Feminine supplies*

* Personal hygiene items*
* Plastic garbage bags, ties (for personal sanitation uses)
* Plastic bucket with tight lid
* Disinfectant
* Household chlorine bleach

Clothing and Bedding
*Include at least one complete change of clothing and footwear per person.
* Sturdy shoes or work boots*
* Rain gear*
* Blankets or sleeping bags*
* Hat and gloves
* Thermal underwear
* Sunglasses

Special Items
* Remember family members with special requirements, such as infants and elderly or disabled persons

For Baby*
* Formula
* Diapers
* Bottles
* Powdered milk
* Medications

For Adults*
* Heart and high blood pressure medication
* Insulin
* Prescription drugs
* Denture needs
* Contact lenses and supplies
* Extra eye glasses

Entertainment
* Games and books

Important Family Documents
* Keep these records in a waterproof, portable container:
  * Will, insurance policies, contracts deeds, stocks and bonds
  * Passports, social security cards, immunization records
  * Bank account numbers

- Credit card account numbers and companies
- Inventory of valuable household goods, important telephone numbers
- Family records (birth, marriage, death certificates)
- Store your kit in a convenient place known to all family members
- Keep a smaller version of the supplies kit in the trunk of your car.
- Keep items in airtight plastic bags.
- Change your stored water supply every six months so it stays fresh.
- Replace your stored food every six months. Re-think your kit and family needs at least once a year.
- Replace batteries, update clothes, etc.
- Ask your physician or pharmacist about storing prescription medications.

To get copies of American Red Cross Community Disaster Education materials, contact your local Red Cross chapter. Information from "Disaster Supplies Kit." developed by the Federal Emergency Management Agency and the American Red Cross.

List of 100 things that might disappear in a crisis

1. Generators (Good ones cost dearly. Gas storage, risky, noisy)
2. Water Filters/Purifiers
3. Portable Toilets
4. Seasoned Firewood. Wood takes about 6 – 12 months to dry for home use.
5. Lamp Oil, Wicks, Lamps (First Choice: Buy CLEAR oil. If scarce, stockpile ANY!)
6. Coleman Fuel. Impossible to stockpile too much.
7. Guns, Ammunition, Pepper Spray, Knives, Clubs, Bats & Slingshots. (for display purposes)
8. Hand-can openers, & hand egg beaters, whisks.
9. Honey/Syrups/white, brown sugar
10. Rice – Beans – Wheat
11. Vegetable Oil (for cooking) Without it food burns/must be boiled etc.,)
12. Charcoal, Lighter Fluid (Will become scarce suddenly)
13. Water Containers (Urgent Item to obtain.) Any size. Small: HARD CLEAR PLASTIC ONLY – (Note: food grade if for drinking).
14. Mini Heater head (Propane) (Without this item, propane won't heat a room.)
15. Grain Grinder (Non-electric)
16. Propane Cylinders (Urgent: Definite shortages will occur).
17. Survival Guide Book.
18. Mantles: Aladdin, Coleman, etc. (Without this item, longer-term lighting is difficult.)
19. Baby Supplies: Diapers/formula. Ointments/aspirin, etc.
20. Washboards, Mop Bucket w/wringer (for Laundry)
21. Cook stoves (Propane, Coleman & Kerosene)
22. Vitamins
23. Propane Cylinder Handle-Holder (Urgent: Small canister use is dangerous without this item)
24. Feminine Hygiene/Hair care/Skin products.
25. Thermal underwear (Tops & Bottoms)
26. Bow saws, axes and hatchets, Wedges (also, honing oil)
27. Aluminum Foil Reg. & Heavy Duty (Great Cooking and Barter Item)
28. Gasoline Containers (Plastic & Metal)
29. Garbage Bags (Impossible To Have Too Many).
30. Toilet Paper, Kleenex, Paper Towels
31. Milk – Powdered & Condensed (Shake Liquid every 3 to 4 months)
32. Garden Seeds (Non-Hybrid) (A MUST)
33. Clothes pins/line/hangers (A MUST)

34. Coleman's Pump Repair Kit

35. Tuna Fish (in oil)

36. Fire Extinguishers (or large box of Baking Soda in every room)

37. First aid kits

38. Batteries (all sizes…buy furthest-out from Expiration Dates)

39. Garlic, spices & vinegar, baking supplies

40. Big Dogs (and plenty of dog food)

41. Flour, yeast & salt

42. Matches. {"Strike Anywhere" preferred.) Boxed, wooden matches will go first

43. Writing paper/pads/pencils, solar calculators

44. Insulated ice chests (good for keeping items from freezing in wintertime.)

45. Work boots, belts, Levis & durable shirts

46. Flashlights/lightsticks & torches, "No. 76 Dietz" Lanterns

47. Journals, Diaries & Scrapbooks (jot down ideas, feelings, experience; Historic Times)

48. Garbage cans Plastic (great for storage, water, transporting – if with wheels)

49. Shampoo, Toothbrush/paste, Mouthwash/floss, nail clippers, etc

50. Cast iron cookware (sturdy, efficient)

51. Fishing supplies/tools

52. Mosquito coils/repellent sprays/creams

53. Duct Tape

54. Tarps/stakes/twine/nails/rope/spikes

55. Candles

56. Laundry Detergent (liquid)

57. Backpacks, Duffel Bags

58. Garden tools & supplies

59. Scissors, fabrics & sewing supplies

60. Canned Fruits, Veggies, Soups, stews, etc.

61. Bleach (plain, **NOT** scented: 4 to 6% sodium hypochlorite)

62. Canning supplies (Jars/lids/wax)

63. Knives & Sharpening tools: files, stones, steel

64. Bicycles…Tires/tubes/pumps/chains, etc

65. Sleeping Bags & blankets/pillows/mats

66. Carbon Monoxide Alarm (battery powered)

67. Board Games, Cards, Dice

68. D-con Rat poison, MOUSE PRUFE II, Roach Killer

69. Mousetraps, Ant traps & cockroach magnets

70. Paper plates/cups/utensils (stock up, folks)

71. Baby wipes, oils, waterless & Antibacterial soap (saves a lot of water)

72. Rain gear, rubberized boots, etc.

73. Shaving supplies (razors & creams, talc, after shave)
74. Hand pumps & siphons (for water and for fuels)
75. Soy sauce, vinegar, bullions/gravy/soup base
76. Reading glasses
77. Chocolate/Cocoa/Tang/Punch (water enhancers)
78. "Survival-in-a-Can"
79. Woolen clothing, scarves/ear-muffs/mittens
80. Boy Scout Handbook, also Leaders Catalog
81. Roll-on Window Insulation Kit (MANCO)
82. Graham crackers, saltines, pretzels, Trail mix/Jerky
83. Popcorn, Peanut Butter, Nuts
84. Socks, Underwear, T-shirts, etc. (extras)
85. Lumber (all types)
86. Wagons & carts (for transport to and from)
87. Cots & Inflatable mattress'
88. Gloves: Work/warming/gardening, etc.
89. Lantern Hangers
90. Screen Patches, glue, nails, screws, nuts & bolts
91. Teas
92. Coffee
93. Cigarettes
94. Wine/Liquors (for bribes, medicinal, etc,)
95. Paraffin wax
96. Glue, nails, nuts, bolts, screws, etc.
97. Chewing gum/candies
98. Atomizers (for cooling/bathing)
99. Hats & cotton neckerchiefs
100. Goats/chickens

Simply cleaning up the mud after a flood may not be sufficient. Contamination depends on other chemicals that might have been in the water, depth and duration of the flood water in the building. Mud may also contain a high density of bacteria.

Volunteer firefighter removes mud from a flooded basement where mold has begun to grow – FEMA photo

U.S. EMERGENCY AGENCY INFORMATION LINKS

NOTE: these links may be changed without notice at any time by the respective states

Alabama http://ema.alabama.gov/CountyEMA/Index.cfm
Alaksa http://www.ak-prepared.com/
Arizona http://www.dem.azdema.gov/
Arkansas http://www.adem.arkansas.gov/
California http://www.oes.ca.gov/
Colorado http://www.dola.state.co.us/dem/index.html
Connecticut http://www.ct.gov/demhs/site/default.asp
Delaware http://dema.delaware.gov/
Florida http://www.floridadisaster.org/
Georgia http://www.gema.ga.gov/
Hawaii http://www.honolulu.gov/dem/
Idaho http://www.bhs.idaho.gov/
Illinois http://www.state.il.us/iema/index.asp
Indiana http://www.in.gov/dhs/
Iowa http://www.iowahomelandsecurity.org/
Kansas http://www.kansas.gov/kdem/
Kentucky http://kyem.ky.gov/
 Louisiana http://gohsep.la.gov/default.aspx
Maine http://www.state.me.us/mema/
Maryland http://www.mema.state.md.us/MEMA/index.jsp
Massachusetts http://www.mass.gov/?pageID=eopshomepage
        &L=1&L0=Home&sid=Eeops
Michigan http://www.michigan.gov/msp/0,1607,7-123- 1593_3507---
,00.html
Minnesota http://www.hsem.state.mn.us/
Mississippi http://www.msema.org/
Missouri http://sema.dps.mo.gov/
Montana http://www.dphhs.mt.gov/PHSD/PHEP-training
        /phep-training-emi.shtml
Nebraska http://www.getting-ready.com/preparedness/
        nebraskaemergencymanagementagencynema.html
Nevada http://www.dem.state.nv.us/
New Hampshire http://www.nh.gov/safety/divisions/hsem/
New Jersey http://www.state.nj.us/njoem/

New Mexico http://www.nmdhsem.org/default.asp?

New York http://www.semo.state.ny.us/
North Carolina http://www.nccrimecontrol.org
North Dakota http://www.nd.gov/des/
Ohio http://ema.ohio.gov/
Oklahoma http://www.ok.gov/oem/
Oregon http://www.oregon.gov/OMD/OEM/
Pennsylvania http://www.pema.state.pa.us/portal/
        server.pt/community/pema_home/4463
Rhode Island http://www.riema.ri.gov/
South Carolina http://www.scemd.org/
South Dakota http://dps.sd.gov/emergency
        _services/emergency_management/default.aspx
Tennessee http://www.tnema.org/
Texas http://www.txdps.state.tx.us/dem/
Utah http://publicsafety.utah.gov/index.html
Vermont http://www.dps.state.vt.us/vem/
Virginia http://www.vdem.state.va.us/
West Virginia http://www.wvdhsem.gov/
Wisconsin http://emergencymanagement.wi.gov/
Wyoming http://wyohomelandsecurity.state.wy.us/main.aspx
FEMA http://www.fema.gov/
Yellowstone Caldera Volcano Observatory
        http://volcanoes.usgs.gov/yvo/
Volcano Precautions
        http://www.volcanolive.com/news.html (very informative
        volcano web site)

        http://volcanoes.usgs.gov/ (volcano hazards program page)

        http://avo.alaska.edu/ (Alaska Redoubt volcano information
        page)
        http://volcanoes.usgs.gov/ash/todo.html (to do lists)

APPENDIX, CASE STUDIES AND OTHER INFORMATION

The Clarksville Tennessee flood of 2010 was an unexpected catastrophe that **rapidly displaced thousands of persons** and destroyed property that was not perceived to be in jeopardy.

<u>NUCLEAR</u> Power Plant incident planning
What exactly should you do if asked to take shelter?

- Go indoors. Close all outside doors and windows. Turn off all air-conditioning or ventilating devices that might draw in outside air.

- Listen to your radio for further instructions. Do not leave your shelter or evacuate unless told to do so.

- If you must go outside to warn a friend or family member, limit your exposure to half an hour or less. Cover your mouth with a cloth while you are outside.

Emergency instructions via radio reports will monitor the status of the emergency. If you go outside and are exposed to a radioactive release from the plant for an extended period of time, instructions might advise you to remove your clothing and take a shower.

What exactly should you do if asked to evacuate?

Once you hear the evacuation order over the radio, follow the authorities instructions.

- Close all doors and windows. Pack a few personal items, and prepare your home as if you were leaving on vacation.

- Position a "NOTIFIED" sign in an easily seen front window or door so authorities will know you have evacuated.

- Follow radio instructions to evacuate to the emergency reception center.

- Drive out of the EPZ by the most direct route before proceeding to the emergency reception center. (See map)

Note: Direct radiation is not fatal in these situations unless the most catastrophic scenario occurs: reactor containment breach, or fuel core meltdown. Residual alpha and beta radiations do pose serious

long term lethal hazards including radiation sickness. Evacuation from the contaminated area is necessary, and the sooner the better.

(this example taken from Sherburn County Minnesota EMA)
http://www.co.sherburne.mn.us/emergencies.php

HURRICANE

EVACUATION PLANNING FACTORS

EXAMPLE #1 HURRICANE ANDREW

Hurricane forecasting is filled with uncertainty.

The National Hurricane Center was unable to accurately predict a landfall 39 hours, much less 51 hours, before landfall. At 5 am Saturday, 48 hours before landfall, Monroe County (Florida Keys) had not yet ordered an evacuation for Andrew because:

- 48 hours out, Hurricane Andrew was barely a Category 1 storm, having just attained Hurricane classification
- It was incorrectly forecasted to move on shore well to the north near Titusville Florida, and then as a Category 2 storm
- It was not forecasted to move ashore for another 72 hours.

EXAMPLE # 2 HURRICANE HARLEY

9 - 14 August 2004 National Hurricane
Center 18 October 2004

Hurricane Charley strengthened rapidly just before striking the southwestern coast of Florida as a Category 4 hurricane on the Saffir-Simpson Hurricane Scale. Charley was the strongest hurricane to hit the United States since Andrew in 1992 and, although small in size, it caused catastrophic wind damage in Charlotte County, Florida. Serious damage occurred well inland over the Florida peninsula.

Hurricane Sandy modifies New Jersey real estate – FEMA photo

EXAMPLE #3 HURRICANE IVAN

2 - 24 September 2004

National Hurricane Center
16 December 2004

Ivan was a classical, long-lived Cape Verde hurricane that reached Category 5 strength three times on the Saffir-Simpson Hurricane Scale (SSHS). It was also the strongest hurricane on record that far south east of the Lesser Antilles. Ivan caused considerable damage and loss of life as it passed through the Caribbean Sea.

NOTE: Government agencies (state, federal) are somewhat capable of action to correct large infrastructure problems, however counties, cities, and municipalities are the front lines when it comes to restoring basic services. Serious disasters will always overwhelm local jurisdictions, thus slowing their effective response. <u>You may be on your own for weeks, months, or years until the areas is rebuilt or you are forced to resettle in another location.</u>

Question: Is the chaos that accompanies disaster expected by governmental agencies?

Answer: YES it is! Planners know they cannot "control" situations, but the public does not appreciate what that means. Readiness means that the jurisdiction has (or has access to) resources that will answer some needs after the disaster has occurred.

EXAMPLE # 4: New Orleans had reviewed the possibility of a hurricane strike.

- November 23, 2004-January 31, 2005: Survey Indicates New Orleans Residents May Not Evacuate In Event of Major Hurricane

"….A poll conducted by the University of New Orleans finds that 62 percent of greater New Orleans' 1.3 million residents would feel safe in their homes during a Category 3 storm. Only in the case of a larger Category 4 or 5 hurricane would a majority of the residents-78 percent-decide to evacuate the city. A total of 401 residents from St. Charles Parish take part in the survey. The figures cause grave concern for the university's researchers who say the results suggest that residents have developed a false sense of security. For decades, residents have successfully rode out moderate-sized hurricanes. But as University of New Orleans pollster Susan Howell explains, Louisiana's dramatic loss of its coastal wetlands means storms will have a greater impact, thus putting the city's residents at greater risk..." [FEMA compilation from Times-Picayune, 6/23/2005; Times-Picayune, 6/23/2005]

NOTES ON TRANSPORTATION, ROUTE PLANNING ETC.

Most city governments know (but few will admit it) that it is really not possible for the government even with National Guard assistance to evacuate all residents:

"**...November 21, 2003**: Study Predicts a Third of New Orleans Residents Would Not Evacuate in Event of Major Hurricane Ivor van Heerden, director of the LSU Center for the Study of the Public Health Impacts of Hurricanes, presents the preliminary findings of a five-year study (see (April 2002)) of the hurricane risk to New Orleans at a special meeting held in the district headquarters of the US Army Corps of Engineers. The preliminary findings indicate that a third of the city's residents would not evacuate in the event of a major hurricane. Of those who do attempt evacuation, many would get stuck in traffic despite plans to use both sides of the highway. The draft findings also indicate that a major hurricane strike on New Orleans would submerge certain parts of the city under as much as 22 feet of water polluted by a mix of oil, gasoline, and other toxic substances released from myriad storage tanks, cars, trucks, flooded homes, stores, and industrial sites during the storm. Wind would cause damage to most buildings, possibly destroying half of them. To mitigate the risk of such a disaster, Van Heerden recommends that federal and state officials revisit two previously rejected proposals to restore the Louisiana coastal wetlands. One of these proposals, which would reroute the Mississippi River to the east of New Orleans, into Breton Sound, had been blocked by shipping interests. The other proposal that should be reconsidered contemplated construction of a barrier wall along the Interstate 10 twin span bridge between eastern New Orleans and the adjacent city of Slidell to reduce the amount of a hurricane storm surge entering the Lake Pontchartrain. [FEMA compilation from Times-Picayune, 11/22/2003]'"

THE MYTH:

- Contemporary weather forecasters using hurricane hunter information and computer modeling can determine where the hurricane will go, and how strong it will be when it makes landfall

- Since the problem has been foreseen, possibly by as much as a week, government responders will be organized and ready to move into the disaster area immediately as the hurricane moves away

- Government planners know how long will be required to evacuate a city and travel to areas of relative safety, and can effectively manage a mass exodus from a large metropolitan area.

- People living in high-risk areas will use common sense, prepare and won't have to make last minute emergency purchases of supplies or fuel. There will be enough supplies for everyone in need.

- Hurricane damage is confined to the near-shore area.

THE REALITY:

- Forecasts only render general direction of hurricanes. Most times they get right but sometimes they are don't . Expect surprises from large storms.

- Hurricanes can and do make unpredictable sharp turns, slow down or speed up.

- Hurricanes also generate severe <u>wind and water</u> <u>damage far inland</u>. Secondary flooding (resulting from rain fall) and tornadoes commonly accompany such storms.

- Government planners operate on a combination of preparation, sound procedures, creative ideas, and hope. They are trained and equipped to work on general situations, not to provide solutions to your personal problems.

From FEMA WEB SITE:
   Evacuation Tips for You and Your
   Family

Release Date: September 11, 2008
Release Number: 3294-009

AUSTIN, Texas -- The state of Texas and Federal Emergency Management Agency (FEMA) advise residents that if evacuation is necessary in your area for the approaching hurricane, it is critical that you and your family respond quickly and responsibly.

Having your own evacuation plan can be a big relief and could help you avoid paying a premium for food, fuel and accommodations and taking a chance on where your family sleeps at night.

Basic Evacuation Planning Steps

Here are three questions you should answer to get started:

1. **Where would you go?** To get out of harm's way, you may need to go north, south, east or west. Pick a destination in each direction. Your primary destination could be with family or friends within the range of one tank full of gas. Stop-and-go driving could drastically reduce how far you can get on a tank of gas, so take that into consideration.

2. **Where would you stay?** If you are with family or friends, certain comforts could be expected. Be sure to discuss this with your hosts ahead of time. Four families in a two bedroom house could be very uncomfortable. If you end up in a shelter, only very basic needs will

be provided, and could be in short supply - but being safe is your first concern.

3. **What would you take with you?** More on this later, but food and water, clothes and comfort and cash and documents are three prime categories. It is recommended that you plan to be self-sustaining for at least three days.

If you don't have reliable transportation of your own, you need to know more in advance about what options are available from your neighbors or local government. Your county emergency manager's office is the source for this information. What you can take with you are the same as above, but you are limited by how much you can carry.

Develop a Detailed Plan
Here is information you will need to know:

- Find out from your local Emergency Management Office about evacuation plans.
- Learn proposed evacuation routes and the locations of potential public shelters.
- If you do not have personal transportation, make arrangements with friends or find out what resources can be provided through your local government.

Develop a Family Communications Plan

- Scale the plan: Do you need to evacuate your neighborhood, your community or the region.
- Share the plan with family members. Discuss what to do if kids are in school, if a parent is far from home, etc.
- Be sure you have all phone numbers: Work, school, cell phones and land lines, host family, friends, your local emergency management office and/or community evacuation resources.

Have your transportation arranged

- Keep your car fueled if evacuation seems likely. Gas stations may be closed during an emergency, out of fuel or unable to pump gas during power outages. Check your oil and other fluids, tire pressure, spare tire, jack and other tools.
- Have a good road map. Evacuation routes may take you on unfamiliar roads.

- If driving with someone else, set meeting place, stay in touch to coordinate pick-up times.
- If using community transportation, find out where and when you need to arrive for pick-up.

Assemble a Disaster Supply Kit

- Food and water for three days and/or special dietary foods.
- Toilet articles (soap, toothbrush, toothpaste, shampoo, etc.)
- Prescription medicines, medical equipment and important medical records.
- Clothing for several days.
- Blankets, pillows, and towels (particularly if you may stay at a public mass care shelter).
- Identification and important papers.
- Checkbook, credit card and cash.
- Flashlights with extra batteries, phone chargers and extra phone batteries.
- Baby or pet supplies including special food, sanitary items and play items.

Prepare to shut down your home or apartment

- Know how to safely shut off electricity, gas and water supplies at main switches and valves.
- Secure all loose yard items like lawn furniture, BBQ grills, bird baths, trash cans, planters, awnings, etc.
- Move valuable items to inner rooms or upper floors.
- Your home could be without power for an extended period.
  - Check your refrigerator and freezer for perishable items.
  - Unplug major appliances to avoid damage from lightning strikes or power surges.
  - Consider obtaining and pre-drilling plywood to board up windows of your home.

What to do if Asked/Told to Evacuate

- Gather all persons in the household together.
- Household members outside the area may be advised not to return during an evacuation. They may be directed to a reception center or mass care shelter where you can join them. They should call you, or you call them, to be sure of everyone's status.
- Board up your home if you decide to cover outside windows.
- Turn off lights and unplug unnecessary appliances.

- Close and lock windows and doors. Close curtains and shades.
- Check with neighbors to see if they need assistance. Offer to share transportation.
- Notify others when you are leaving and where you plan to go.
- Load your Disaster Supply kit and all who are traveling together and leave.
- Do not call local fire or police departments for information. Emergency workers need their lines for emergency use. If you need special help, call your local Emergency Management Office.
- If you need a ride, go with a neighbor or contact your local Emergency Management Office.

More information about this disaster is available online at www.fema.gov or www.txdps.state.tx.us/dem FEMA coordinates the federal government's role in preparing for, preventing, mitigating the effects of, responding to, and recovering from all domestic disasters, whether natural or man-made, including acts of terror.

FEMA 500 C Street SW, Washington, D.C. 20472
Disaster Assistance: (800) 621-FEMA

FLOOD

The following are important points to remember when driving in flood conditions:

During a flood

- Six inches of water will reach the bottom of most passenger cars causing loss of control and possible stalling.
- A foot of water will float many vehicles.
- Two feet of rushing water can carry away most vehicles including sport utility vehicles (SUV's) and pick-ups.

After a Flood

- Listen for news reports to learn whether the community's water supply is safe to drink.

- Avoid flood waters; water may be contaminated by oil, gasoline, or raw sewage. Water may also be electrically charged from underground or downed power lines.

- Avoid moving water.

- Be aware of areas where flood waters have receded. Roads may have weakened and could collapse under the weight of a car.

- Stay away from downed power lines, and report them to the power company.

- Return home only when authorities indicate it is safe.

- Stay out of any building if it is surrounded by flood waters.

- Use extreme caution when entering buildings; there may be hidden damage, particularly in foundations.

- Service damaged septic tanks, cesspools, pits, and leaching systems as soon as possible. Damaged sewage systems are serious health hazards.

- Clean and disinfect <u>everything that got wet</u>. Mud left from floodwater can contain sewage and chemicals.

Once an automobile has been immersed in water, it is basically destroyed and will forever show the signs, (and smells) of the damage.

Hurricane Sandy
Official evacuation order – City of New York 2012
Note highlighted passages, and multiple departments that
are directed to act

THE CITY OF NEW YORK
OFFICE OF THE MAYOR
NEW YORK, N. Y. 10007

EXECUTIVE ORDER NO. 163
PROCLAMATION OF A STATE OF EMERGENCY AND
EVACUATION ORDER
October 28,2012

WHEREAS, the National Weather Service is predicting that a
hurricane or tropical storm may hit the City within hours; and
WHEREAS, the Governor has issued a Declaration of Emergency
for the State of New York, including the City of New York and
contiguous counties;
§ 1. Pursuant to the powers vested in me by the laws of the State of
New York and the City of New York, including but not limited to
the New York Executive Law, the Charter and Administrative
Code of the City of New York, and the common law authority to
protect the public in the event of an emergency, I hereby declare a
State of Emergency.
§ 2. This State of Emergency has been declared because
anticipated weather conditions are likely to cause heavy flooding,
power outages, and disruption of public transportation and other
vital services, and **these conditions imperil the public safety.**
§ 3. The Office of Emergency Management, Police Department,
Fire Department, Department of Health and Mental Hygiene,
Health and Hospitals Corporation, Department of Sanitation,
Department of Housing Preservation and Development,
Department of Sanitation, Department of Buildings, Department of
Environmental Protection, Department of Transportation, New
York City Housing Authority, Department of Housing
Preservation and Development, Department of Design and
Construction, Department of Homeless Services, Department of

Correction, Department of Parks and Recreation, Department of Citywide Administrative Services, Office of Citywide Event Coordination and Management, Office of Labor Relations, School Construction Authority, Department of Education, Department of Information Technology and Telecommunications, Department for the Aging, Department of Small Business Services, Department of Consumer Affairs, Office of Media and Entertainment and Department of Cultural Affairs, Taxi and Limousine Commission, and other relevant departments and agencies, are directed, by and through themselves and others as needed, to undertake whatever activities and measures are needed, including revocation of street activity and other related event permits, to protect life and property or bring the emergency situation under control.

§ 4. All members of the public (other than authorized government personnel and essential emergency personnel, and patients and residents of hospitals, nursing homes and senior homes) are **ordered to evacuate their homes and businesses if they are located in Zone A, as defined by the Office of Emergency Management.** Members of the public are ordered to evacuate Zone A no later than 7:00 p.m. on Sunday, October 28.2012.

§ 5. Following evacuation from Zone A, **all members of the public (other than authorized government personnel and essential emergency personnel) shall remain outside of Zone A.**

§ 6. **Any person who knowingly violates any provision of this Order is guilty of a class B misdemeanor.**

§ 7. **This Order shall take effect immediately. It shall remain in effect for five (5) days unless it is terminated or modified at an earlier date.**

Michael Bloomberg
Mayor

EARTHQUAKE, VOLCANO, AND ASSOCIATED EVENTS
Tectonic plate behavior (USGS)

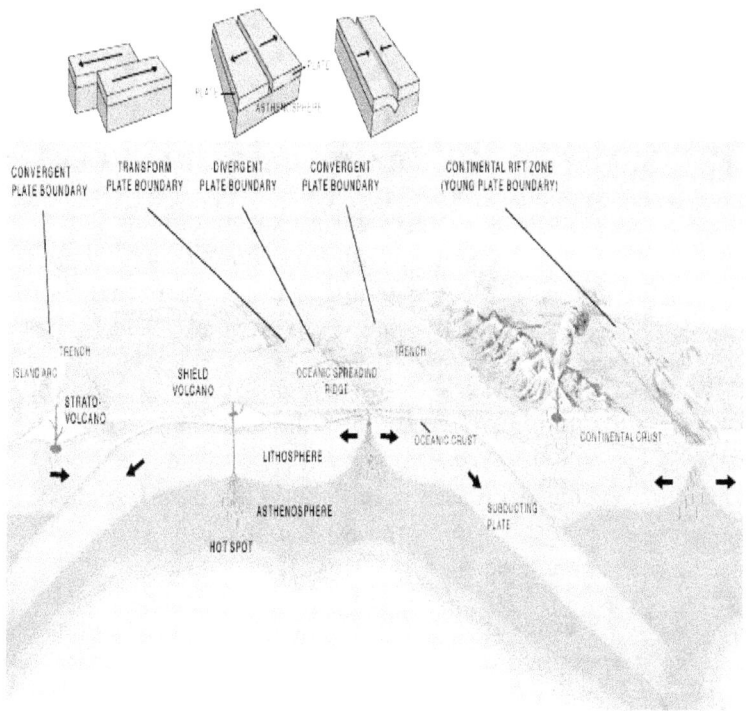

VOLCANO

Table 1. **SUMMARY OF VOLCANO ALERT LEVELS**	
NORMAL	Volcano is in typical background, non-eruptive state or, *after a change from a higher level,* volcanic activity has ceased and volcano has returned to non-eruptive background state.
ADVISORY	Volcano is exhibiting signs of elevated unrest above known background level or, *after a change from a higher level,* volcanic activity has decreased significantly but continues to be closely monitored for possible renewed increase.
WATCH	Volcano is exhibiting heightened or escalating unrest with increased potential of eruption, timeframe uncertain, **OR** eruption is underway but poses limited hazards.
WARNING	Hazardous eruption is imminent, underway, or suspected.

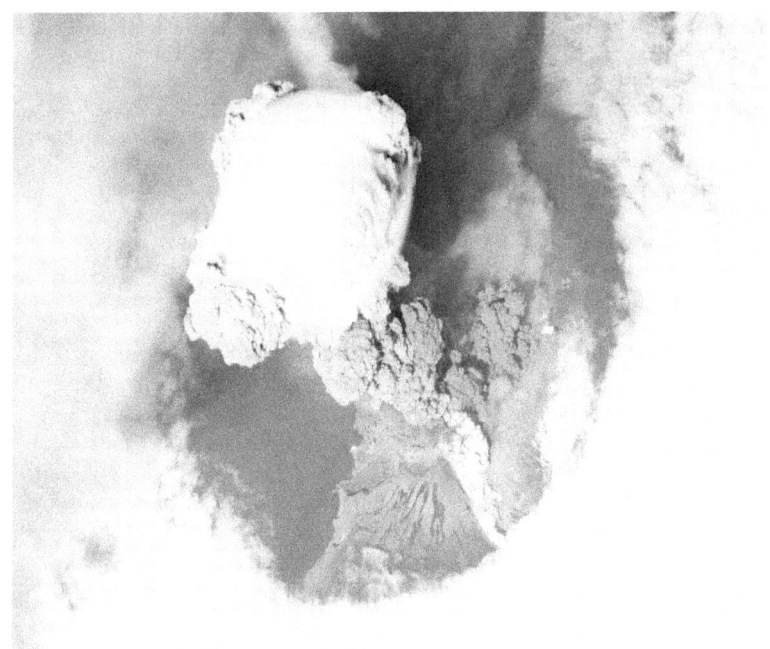

Astronaut's view of a volcanic explosion similar to the ones that occur on Montserrat. Sarychev Peak Eruption, June 2009, Kuril Islands (NE of Japan). Note the PFs radiating from its base (NASA).

What To Do If A Volcano Erupts, Volcanic Ash fall - How to be Prepared for an Ash fall, How to protect your home, car, children, and pets

Washington State Military Department, Emergency Management Division, and the USGS Cascades Volcano Observatory, 1999   What is Volcanic Ash ?

Volcanic ash is rock that has been pulverized into dust or sand by volcanic activity. In very large eruptions, ash is accompanied by rocks having the weight and density of hailstones. Volcanic ash is hot near the volcano, but it is cool when it falls at greater distances. Ash fall blocks sunlight, reducing visibility and sometimes causing darkness. Ash fall can be accompanied by lightning.

(Above) In general, surfaces should be vacuumed to remove as much ash as possible from carpets, furniture, office equipment, appliances, and other items. Portable vacuum systems equipped with high-efficiency particulate filtering systems are recommended whenever possible. The severity of ash intrusion depends on the integrity of windows and entrances, the air intake features, and the care exercised to control the transport of ash into a building or home via shoes and clothing. Care should also be taken to avoid further contamination during the emptying, cleaning, and maintenance of vacuum equipment. In hot climates, where windows are permanently open, or absent, clean up of houses may be needed several times per day. Clean up inside should only be undertaken after the outside areas have been well cleared (USGS photo).

Fresh volcanic ash is gritty, abrasive, sometimes corrosive, and always unpleasant. Although ash is not highly toxic, it can trouble infants, the elderly and those with respiratory ailments. Small ash particles can abrade the front of the eye under windy and ashy conditions.

Ash abrades and jams machinery. It contaminates and clogs ventilation, water supplies and drains. Ash also causes electrical short circuits -- in transmission lines (especially when wet), in computers, and in microelectronic devices. Power often goes out during and after ash fall.

Long-term exposure to wet ash can corrode metal. (exposure to ash can cause respiratory distress or complete respiratory collapse-death)

Ash accumulates like heavy snowfall, but doesn't melt. The weight of ash can cause roofs to collapse. A one-inch layer of ash weighs 5-10 pounds per square foot when dry, but 10-15 pounds per square foot when wet. Wet ash is slippery. Ash re-suspended by wind, and human activity, and can disrupt lives for months after an eruption.

What to do in case of an ash fall

Oregon Department of Geology and Mineral Industries (web site**)**
800 NE Oregon St.
Portland, OR 97232
(971) 673-1555

GENERAL PRINCIPLES

- Know in advance what to expect and how to deal with it; that will make it manageable.
- In ashy areas, use dust masks and eye protection. If you don't have a dust mask, use a wet handkerchief.

- As much as possible, keep ash out of buildings, machinery, air and water supplies, downspouts, storm drains, etc.
- Stay indoors to minimize exposure -- especially if you have respiratory ailments.
- Minimize travel -- driving in ash is hazardous to you and your car.
- Don't tie up phone line with non-emergency calls.
- Use your radio for information on the ash fall.

What to do <u>before</u> an ash fall
Whether in a car, at home, at work or play, you should always be prepared. Intermittent ash fall and re-suspension of ash on the ground may continue for years.

YOUR HOME
Keep these items in your home in case of any natural hazards emergency:
- Extra dust masks.
- Enough non-perishable food for at least three days.
- Enough drinking water for at least three days (one gallon per person per day).
- Plastic wrap (to keep ash out of electronics).
- First aid kit and regular medications.
- Battery-operated radio with extra batteries.
- Lanterns or flashlights with extra batteries.
- Extra wood, if you have a fireplace or wood stove.
- Extra blankets and warm clothing.
- Cleaning supplies (broom, vacuum, shovels, etc.).
- Small amount of extra cash (ATM machines may not be working).

YOUR CHILDREN

- Explain what a volcano is and what they should expect and do if ash falls.
- Know your school's emergency plan.
- Have quiet games and activities available.

YOUR PETS

- Store extra food and drinking water.
- Keep extra medicine on hand.
- Keep your animals under cover, if possible.

YOUR CAR

Any vehicle can be considered a movable, second home. Always carry a few items in your vehicle in case of delays, emergencies, or mechanical failures.

<u>Vehicle Mitigation Techniques:</u>

- Increase maintenance, oil change, etc.; interval will depend on degree of exposure.
- Extend air intakes (use dryer vent hose) farther above ground.
- Seal air filter with spot welds and/or silicon sealer; add air hose to external, truck-type filter; seal all connections.
- Purge-lube all joints, bearings, etc.
- Use pre-filters: polyester batting, oil-soaked foam rubber, rubberized foam slip-on filters (like a shower cap; cheap and disposable).
- Seal crankcase; use positive seals on dipstick. Gasoline engines are less susceptible to oil contamination due to positive pressure of PCV system. Diesels may be more vulnerable to ash: no PCV; supercharged; crankcase and transmission vents open.
- Wash vehicle and engine to remove ash.
- Install fuel filters, 70 gallons of gas means 70 gallons of contaminated air as tank empties. Maintain positive pressure in cab/interior by keeping heater on. Do not lead engine air intake hose into car interior; an engine will draw in up to 200ft of air per minute at freeway speeds.

Other necessary supplies

- Dust masks and eye protection.
- Blankets and extra clothing.
- Emergency food and drinking water.
- General emergency supplies: first aid kit, flashlight, fire extinguisher, tool kit, flares, matches, survival manual, etc.
- Waterproof tarp, heavy tow rope.
- Extra air and oil filters, extra oil, windshield wiper blades and windshield washer fluid.
- Cell phone with extra battery.

What to do <u>during and after</u> an ash fall
- Minimize driving and other activities that stir ash.
- Remove as much ash as you can from frequently used areas. Clean from the top down. Wear a dust mask.

- Prior to sweeping, dampen ash to ease removal. Be careful to not wash ash into drainpipes, sewers, storm drains, etc.
- Use water sparingly. Widespread use of water for clean-up may deplete public water supply.
- Maintain protection for dust-sensitive items (e.g, computers, machinery) until the environment is really ash-free.
- Seek advice from public officials regarding disposal of volcanic ash in your community.
- Wet ash can be slippery. Use caution when climbing on ladders and roofs.
- Establish childcare to assist parents involved in cleanup.

SEM image provided by A.M. Sarna-Wojcicki Tic marks 100 microns apart – courtesy USGS

Parting thoughts:

We hope that this book has helped point the direction and encouraged you to help yourself now.

Although our focus is evacuation, these principles will also be useful in all your general preparedness efforts. In this time of uncertainty and rising chaos, none of us should blindly entrust our family's safety to an impersonal agency or government, however well equipped and well intentioned they may be. Challenges will come, and conditions will surely change.

Be vigilant, be well informed, be prepared, follow through, and remain committed. Remember that "if you are prepared, you will not fear!"